# A note from the auth

‖‖‖‖‖‖‖‖‖‖‖‖‖‖‖‖
W9-CJZ-103

It's unbelieveable to think that many years ago I wrote the first version of "A Fresh Approach to the Snare Drum" with a pen and blank staff paper – and 25 years later, this book has been used by over 200,000 beginners just like you! Out of those thousands of students who have used it, many have become professional players and teachers. It goes to show you that if you have patience and are willing to work hard, soon you'll have a great foundation of technique, reading ability and musicianship that you'll be able to use – whether you want to play in the school band or eventually become a professional drummer, percussionist or educator!

A LOT has changed over the past 25 years – and now it's more fun than ever to learn to play the snare drum. As you work through the book, be sure to check out the **FREE VIDEO LESSONS** that are available on YouTube. In each lesson, I'll demonstrate each new technique, count each new rhythm and give you tons of pointers that'll help you along the way. Go to **www.youtube.com/user/FreshApproachBooks** or search for "Fresh Approach to Snare Drum YouTube Playlist" on Google.

For the band director using this method to teach beginning percussionists, the free YouTube lessons can be an invaluable source of information in preparation for your class. Or with a computer and projector, you can bring me into your classroom to help teach your percussionists – or reinforce the information you're providing to them.

As you learn new each new line, be sure to utilize the playalong tracks on the **DATA CD** that is included with this book. On this disc, you'll find folders with mp3 files that you can load on your computer or portable device. Use the slow-medium-fast practice tracks to learn each line separately – then you can play them along with cool accompaniments that utilize musical styles from around the world!

Finally, in the back of this new edition of the book is *a step-by-step guide for the beginning drumset player!* I encourage you to learn to play the drumset because not only is it fun, but you'll also apply all the techniques that you've learned to another VERY important instrument in the percussion family.

I sincerely hope that you'll enjoy using this book and that it'll be the beginning to a lifelong love of drumming – and to music. Good luck in your endeavor to learn to play the snare drum!

*Mark W....*

## This book is dedicated to Lynn, Kaitlyn and Drew.

*Also, a quick "thank-you" to my daughter Kaitlyn for posing for the photos in the introduction – and for allowing her dad to teach her to play the drums. You've come a long way, baby!*

For information on other products from Mark Wessels Publications, or to order additional copies of "A Fresh Approach to the Snare Drum," please visit us online:

### Mark Wessels Publications

*http://www.mwpublications.com*

"A Fresh Approach to the Snare Drum" by Mark Wessels
International Copyright Secured • 1994 • All Rights Reserved
No portion of this book may be photocopied or reproduced in any way without permission from the author.

# Learn About the Snare Drum and Sticks

Before you grab the sticks and start playing, take a few minutes to learn about your new instrument! There are several free video lessons on YouTube where I describe the parts of the drum, show you how to set up your percussion kit and give you step-by-step instructions on how to tune your drum.

Find the FREE video lessons here:
www.youtube.com/user/FreshApproachBooks

Batter (top) Head

Counter Hoop (rim)

Tension Rod (lug)

Rod (lug) Casing

Snare Strainer (throw–off)

Shell

Snares

Snare (bottom) Head

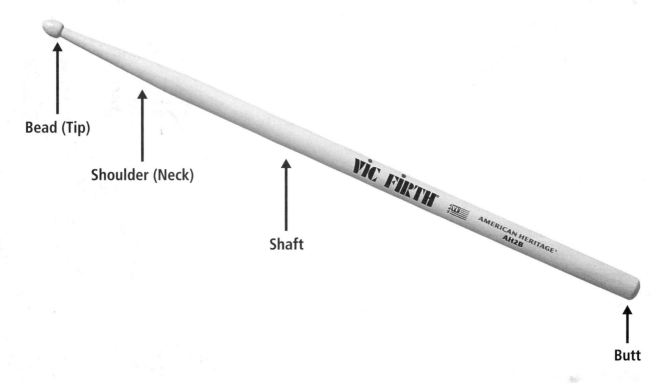

Bead (Tip)

Shoulder (Neck)

Shaft

Butt

VIC FIRTH

AMERICAN HERITAGE
AH2B

# The Matched Grip

The matched grip is most commonly used by percussionists because it immediately applies to all other percussion instruments. I recommend that all beginning students start with matched grip because of the relative ease that young students have learning to play with two hands that grip the stick and move in exactly the same manner. Here are the steps to achieving a perfect matched grip.

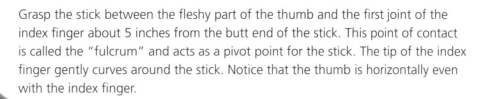

Grasp the stick between the fleshy part of the thumb and the first joint of the index finger about 5 inches from the butt end of the stick. This point of contact is called the "fulcrum" and acts as a pivot point for the stick. The tip of the index finger gently curves around the stick. Notice that the thumb is horizontally even with the index finger.

Lightly wrap the remaining three fingers around the stick. Avoid squeezing the stick unnecessarily!

The proper playing position can be achieved by first standing without the sticks in your hands. Allow your arms to hang loosely by your sides and your shoulders to relax.

Lift your forearms until they are slightly below parallel to the floor. Notice that the hands are naturally flat (or almost flat) and that the elbows are in a relaxed position, a few inches from your sides. You'll want to keep this natural space between the hands.

The positioning of your snare drum or practice pad is very important! Adjust the height of the drum so that the top rim is 4 inches below your belly button (about a hand's width). As you pull the sticks up to playing position, check to see if the forearms are in the correct position (slightly below parallel), then make slight adjustments from there.

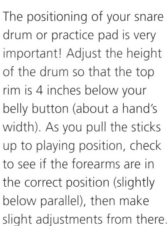

Bring both sticks up, placing the tips in the center of the drum. Your hands should be close to flat, and the sticks should be at about a 90° angle. Compare yourself in a mirror to these pictures of the matched grip. If everything looks good, then you are now ready to learn the stroke!

# The Traditional Left Hand Grip

The traditional grip was developed many years ago at a time when drummers wore their instruments hanging on the side of the body. With this drum position, it made sense to use this left hand grip – but today, it's much easier to learn to play with matched grip.

Because the traditional grip involves an entirely different grip from right to left, as well as using different stroke motions with dissimilar muscle groups, I recommend that all beginners start with the matched grip and "switch over" to traditional ONLY after the fundamentals of the matched stroke are developed. If you are just starting out and still wish to learn the traditional grip, be patient and persistent to develop the proper technique.

Start with the arm hanging by your side, shoulder relaxed.

Pick up your forearm, maintaining the relaxed hand position, with the thumbnail facing up. You should always be able to look down and see your thumbnail!

Open your hand as if holding an imaginary tennis ball (fig. A). Lay the stick in the crotch of the hand, about four inches from the butt. The shaft of the stick will rest just above the cuticle of the ring finger – between the knuckle and where the fingernail begins (fig. B). Wrap the index finger around the stick and place the pad of the thumb on the side of the first knuckle (fig. C). The middle finger rests lightly on the stick and the picky curves under to provide support for the ring finger.

**Figure A**     **Figure B**     **Figure C**

As you move the stick into playing position, remember to point the thumbnail toward the ceiling. Check your grip and playing position in a mirror.

# The Rebound Stroke

When playing the snare drum, there are 5 types of strokes, or ways that you will strike the drum with the stick. The first stroke you'll learn is called the REBOUND stroke, named for the way that the stick is allowed to naturally REBOUND when it strikes the drum head.

Bring the stick to the "up" position by bending right wrist up until the stick is perpendicular to the floor. The forearm might raise slightly, but make sure that the elbow stays close to the body. Allow a little space between the palm of the hand and the fingers. Relax the wrists and fingers – don't squeeze the stick!

The motion that you'll use to produce the rebound stroke is similar to bouncing a basketball. When you throw a basketball to the floor, it will naturally rebound – no energy is required other than the initial toss. Start with your stick in the up position and "throw" it towards the drum. As the stick strikes the head, allow it to REBOUND naturally – pushing the wrist and hand back to the up position. If you throw the stick with enough velocity (speed), the energy of the rebound push your hand back up. DO NOT PULL THE STICK BACK UP! Let the rebound do all the work!

During the rebound stroke, keep the fulcrum in tact, with the back fingers resting lightly on the stick. Remember to stay as relaxed as possible.

## One Hand Exercise

To master the rebound stroke, you must train your muscles to respond in the same way every time, whether you're thinking about it or not. We refer to this as "muscle memory."

To train your muscles to make a perfect rebound stroke, set a metronome on '60' and play right hand strokes for 2 minutes – then repeat the exercise with the metronome set at 80 beats per minute, 100 and 120.

Watch yourself in a mirror to constantly check your grip and path of the stick. Concentrate on feeling the motion of the stick. Allow it to rebound naturally without any tension in your arms, wrists, hands and fingers. Matched grip players should repeat this exercise on the left hand, paying attention to the same details as the right.

## Left Hand Traditional Stroke

For the traditional grip player, the left hand stroke is completely different than the right hand, though the concept of the rebound stroke is exactly the same. The "up" position of the left hand is created by "turning the wrist" on the axis of the forearm, similar to turning a door-knob. It is very important to note that the stick motion of the left hand is made BY ROTATING THE WRIST – not by lifting the forearm!

Using the same rebound concept described above, start in the up position and "throw" the stick to the drum. As the stick rebounds, allow the energy to rotate the stick back to the up position – DON'T LIFT IT BACK UP! Stay as relaxed as possible in the wrists and fingers, making sure that the contact point of the thumb and index finger remains in tact. Allow the stick some "wiggle" room between the index finger and middle finger if that helps you to relax the hand (but don't take the back three fingers completely off the stick)!

Repeat the "One Hand Exercise" on the left hand. This is were patience and discipline is required! The left hand traditional grip is usually very awkward for a length of time because you are working muscle groups that are rarely used in normal day–to–day activity.

**A SPECIAL NOTE:**
There is no substitue for a professional drum instructor! I highly recommend that you find a teacher in your area, especially early in your drumming career. Call local music stores or the music department at a local university for recommendations.

# LESSON 1

## Technique WORKOUT

Our first technique exercise is called **"8 on a hand"** and reinforces the proper REBOUND STROKES that you learned in the previous exercise, only this time with 8 strokes on the right, followed by 8 on the left.

Practice this exercise with the accompaniment MP3 tracks in the Lesson 1 folder on the DATA CD – or play along with a metronome set at 160, 180 and 200. As you work your way through the book, practicing with these tracks or with a metronome will help you to develop a steady TEMPO.

*Watch the videos for this lesson here:*
www.youtube.com/user/FreshApproachBooks

R   R   R   R      R   R   R   R      L   L   L   L      L   L   L   L

After working on rebound strokes in the "8 on a hand" exercise, you can add the "4-2-1" exercise notated in the TECHNIQUE WORKOUT section of the book on page 73.

## Snare Drum RUDIMENT:

## Single Stroke Roll

The snare drum **rudiments** are a collection of the fundamental skills and techniques necessary to becoming a successful percussionist. Mastering the rudiments will take many years of practice and practicing them EVERYDAY is important if you want to develop into a great drummer! Included with this book is a rudiment POSTER, which includes all 40 essential rudiments.

Our first rudiment is called the Single Stroke Roll– or ALTERNATING SINGLE STROKES. The goal on this rudiment is not to produce a "drum roll", but rather to play perfect alternating rebound strokes. Over the course of the 20 lessons in this book, we'll gradually increase the tempo until it begins to sound like a roll!

Practice this rudiment with the BRONZE LEVEL Single Stroke Roll rudiment playalong track, located in the "Rudiments" folder on the DATA CD.

R   L   R   L      R   L   R   L      R   L   R   L      R   L   R   L

Also practice starting on the left. Starting with the "weak hand" increases your ability to make every stroke sound the same.

L   R   L   R      L   R   L   R      L   R   L   R      L   R   L   R

## Snare Drum RUDIMENT:

## Double Stroke Roll

Again, we'll learn this rudiment at a slow tempo, playing ALTERNATING DOUBLE STROKES. Work to ensure that every stroke sounds exactly the same, practicing along with the BRONZE LEVEL Double Stroke Roll playalong track. Only play up to the speed where you can stay relaxed and comfortable.

R   R   L   L      R   R   L   L      R   R   L   L      R   R   L   L

If you're right-handed, leading with the left will strengthen your weaker hand.

L   L   R   R      L   L   R   R      L   L   R   R      L   L   R   R

On page 72 & 78, I've included **LESSON PROGRESS CHARTS** to help you track the tempos of the essential exercises and rudiments that you'll learn as we progress through the book. Refer to this chart frequently as a guide for your weekly progress!

Start these sticking exercises with a metronome set on 120, playing each line separately for two minutes. Then try all 10 lines without stopping, repeating each line twice. After you can play all ten with consistent rebound strokes and no mistakes, move the metronome up to 140 and repeat the process. Once you reach 180, you're ready to play along with the accompaniment MP3 track!

**❶** R  R  R  R    R  R  R  R    L  L  L  L    L  L  L  L

**❷** R  R  R  R    L  L  L  L    R  R  R  R    L  L  L  L

**❸** R  R  L  L    R  R  L  L    R  R  L  L    R  R  L  L

**❹** R  L  R  L    R  L  R  L    R  L  R  L    R  L  R  L

**❺** R  L  R  R    L  R  L  L    R  L  R  R    L  R  L  L

**❻** R  R  L  R    L  L  R  L    R  R  L  R    L  L  R  L

**❼** R  L  L  R    L  R  R  L    R  L  L  R    L  R  R  L

**❽** R  R  R  L    R  R  R  L    R  R  R  L    R  R  R  L

**❾** L  L  L  R    L  L  L  R    L  L  L  R    L  L  L  R

**❿** R  L  R  L    R  R  L  L    R  L  R  L    R  R  L  L

**HOT TIP:**
If you have problems playing a line without mistakes, slow down! If you practice it correctly at a slow tempo, you'll learn it much quicker than by making repeated mistakes.

---

Before we start reading music, here are a few musical terms you need to memorize:

**Essential Musical Terms**

### Staff:

5 lines and 4 spaces

### Bar Lines:

Divides the staff into measures

### Measure:

Space between two bar lines

### Double Bar:

Marks the end of a section

### Quarter Note & Rest:

Tells when to play or rest

### Time Signature:
Top number tells **how many beats are in one measure**

Bottom number tells **what kind of note receives one beat**

*Don't miss out on the free videos for all the lessons in this book!* ☞
www.youtube.com/user/FreshApproachBooks

# LESSON 2

**Technique WORKOUT**

It is important to develop a daily regime of practice on technique exercises and rudiments in order to develop good fundamentals. For this lesson, practice exercise #1 and #2 on page 73 for at least one full minute at mm=90 (double time) and the single stroke and double stroke roll rudiments with the BRONZE level rudiment playalong.

**Fill in the Blanks!**

Fill in the blanks to provide the definition for each time signature.

❶ **3/4** There are _____ beats in each _____
The _____ _____ receives one beat

❷ **2/4** _____
_____

❸ Draw five quarter notes and 5 quarter rests

❹ When you count quarter notes or rests, you will always start on count "one" for the first note or rest in the measure. Write the counts in under the notes and above the rests in the following measures. Watch the time signatures!

**Special Note:**

Before you begin the Playing Exercises, you may wish to practice the special exercises that are included in the **Appendix** on page 54 in the back of this book. These drills are provided for extra practice on the new material covered in each lesson.

**Playing Exercises**

Practice counting each exercise out loud to a metronome before you play. Stay relaxed and use alternating rebound strokes. PRACTICE tracks are available for each line to help you work them up at slow, medium and fast tempos. After you've worked up each line separately, try playing along with the ACCOMPANIMENT track!

**HOT TIP:**
Try tapping your foot while you play. This will not only help you to keep a steady tempo, but it will also develop the necessary hand to foot coordination required to play the drumset!

As you play through these lines, think of "playing your foot" on the quarter rests!

❶

❷

❸

❹

❺

**HOT TIP:**

If you make a mistake while playing along with the MP3, stop and start over again. Practicing mistakes develops bad habits!

**Snare Drum Rudiment:**

**Multiple Bounce Roll**

The second type of stroke that you will learn is called the BOUNCE stroke. If you've ever heard a "drum roll," then already know the type of sound that a multiple bounce produces!

Using only one motion, strike the drum and add pressure to the stick at the fulcrum to start the stick bouncing. As the stick bounces, gradually RELEASE the pressure to lengthen the bounce. Try to develop a long multiple bounce by playing several on each hand (notated with a "z" through the note stem):

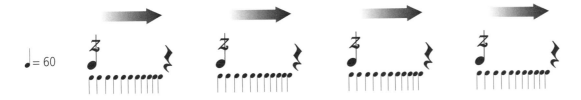

After you've developed great multiple bounces on each hand separately, learn Exercise #3 on page 73.

**Playing Exercises**

Go back through this lesson and bounce all of the quarter notes in the first 6 lines (quarter note = 60). When you can produce a good sounding "buzzzzzzzz" on each stroke, bounce the quarter notes with an "z" in the following exercise and duet. Try to make each bounce "bleed" into the next stroke.

**HOT TIP:**

Practice with the Mutiple Bounce Roll BRONZE LEVEL MP3 track each day. If you're right handed, start on your left hand!

**The Downstroke**

The **DOWNSTROKE** (or "controlled stroke") is the third of 5 strokes for the snare drum. It is used to stop the stick from rebounding off the drumhead. Start with the hand in the up position, then strike the drum just as you would a rebound stroke. At the moment the stick makes contact with the head, stop the rebound with a little pressure in the back fingers – then immediately RELAX the fingers after the stick stops.

In order to learn this important stroke properly, I HIGHLY RECCOMMEND that you watch the video lesson available on YouTube!

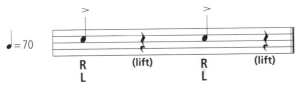

Repeat several times on each hand to develop the DOWNSTROKE

**HOT TIP:**

Don't try to strike the drum harder to produce a downstroke. The height of the stick and weight of the wrist & forearm will take care of the volume.

# LESSON 3

| | |
|---|---|
| **Technique WORKOUT** | It is imortant to begin each practice session with the technique exercises and rudiments suggested on page 72 & 78. In this lesson, you will add exercise #4 which helps you to develop smooth, relaxed double strokes. Practice the double strokes on each hand separately (Ex. A), then alternating (Ex. B). |

**The 8th Note**

An eighth note looks similar to a quarter note, but with one "flag" attached to the stem. Practice drawing 5 eighth notes on this musical staff:

You will often see eighth notes connected together in PAIRS. In this case, instead of a "flag," the two stems are connected together with a BEAM. Draw 3 more PAIRS of 8th notes on this staff:

    There are two 8th notes in one quarter note.

**MUSIC MATH:**   Fill in the correct number in the blank. Remember that there are TWO 8th notes for each quarter.

1. One ♩ = ____ ♪'s       2. Two ♩'s = ____ ♪'s       3. Five ♩'s = ____ ♪'s

4. Two ♪'s = ____ ♩'s       5. Four ♪'s = ____ ♩'s       6. Ten ♪'s = ____ ♩'s

When counting in quarter time, the quarter notes fall on the "downbeats" (counts 1, 2, 3, etc.). The first 8th note in a pair also falls on the downbeat – the second falls on the "upbeat" and is called "and" or "te."

| | | | | | | | | | | | |
|---|---|---|---|---|---|---|---|---|---|---|---|
| 1 | 2 | 3 & 4 | | 1 | 2 & 3 | 4 | | 1 & 2 & 3 | 4 | | |
| 1 | 2 | 3 te 4 | | 1 | 2 te 3 | 4 | | 1 te 2 te 3 | 4 | | |

**Repeat Signs**

Two dots place before a double bar 〔:‖〕 is called a **repeat sign.** When you reach a repeat sign, go back to the similar sign: 〔‖:〕 If no similar sign is indicated, go back and play from the beginning.

**Key Exercises**

Count each exercise out loud to a metronome set on 80 first. The "downbeats" (right hands) should always fall with the metronome clicks. Any 8th note on the "upbeat" (or left hand) will fall between the beats. After you work up each Key Exercise, learn the **Lesson 3 Appendix** on page 55 and 56 before moving on the the Playing Exercises.

**HOT TIP:**

Learn each of these Key Exercises separately with the PRACTICE tracks before attempting the ACCOMPANIMENT track.

**A**

R   R   R      R L R L R L R L

**B**

R   R   R      R L R   R L R

**C**

R   R L R   R L R   R   R

**D**

R L R L R   R      R L R L R   R

The **upstroke** is a preparation stroke for the downstroke and is responsible for the "flow" of rudimental accent patterns. To produce an upstroke, play a soft wrist stroke, then immediately lift the hand to the "up" position. The upstroke will position the hand for the following downstroke in these short exercises:

## The Upstroke

**HOT TIP:**
Be sure to watch the video lesson on YouTube for this important stroke!

Watch for REPEAT SIGNS in these exercises. After working up each line, go back and "buzz" the 8th notes.

## Playing Exercises

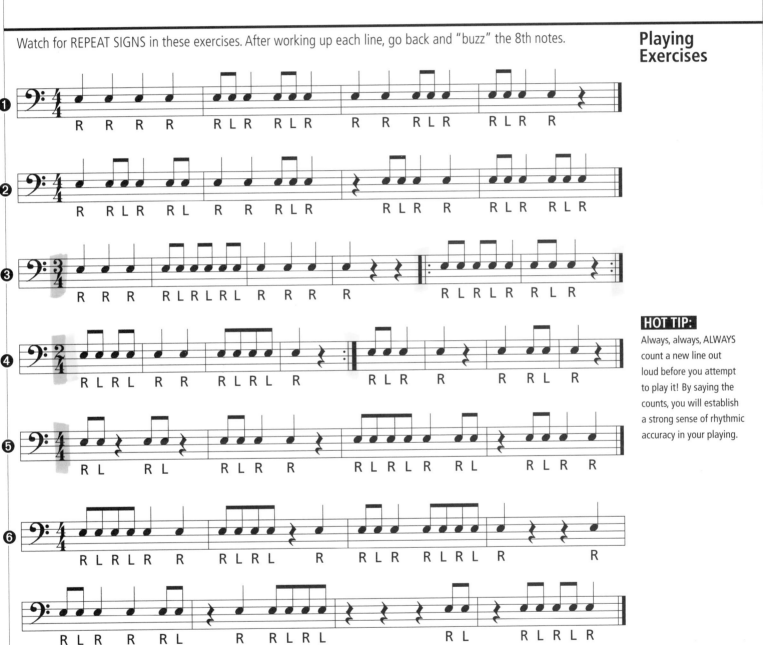

**HOT TIP:**
Always, always, ALWAYS count a new line out loud before you attempt to play it! By saying the counts, you will establish a strong sense of rhythmic accuracy in your playing.

The 5 stroke roll consists of two double strokes, followed by an accent. In the first example, play the "slashed" 8th notes marked as MULTIPLE BOUNCES. In the second, play the slashed 8th notes as DOUBLE STROKES.

## Snare Drum Rudiment:

## The Five Stroke Roll

# LESSON 4

## Technique WORKOUT

Stay on track with the technique exercises and rudiments by referring to the progress chart on page 72 & 78! If you cannot keep up with the tempo marked on each exercise in Lesson 4, spend more time on your fundamentals each day.

## Single Stroke Four

The Single Stroke Four is a new RUDIMENT that will increase your speed on rebound strokes. Its name explains how rudiment is played because it's made up of four single strokes! In order to play this rudiment, you should also learn how to "vocalize" it:

| Say this: | "DIG | a | da | dah " | | " DIG | a | da | dah " |
|---|---|---|---|---|---|---|---|---|---|
| Play this: | R | L | R | L | | R | L | R | L |
| or this: | L | R | L | R | | L | R | L | R |

## Coordination Exercise

This exercise is for one player. The right hand plays the bottom notes on the rim while the left hand plays the top notes on the drum head. After you work it up, switch hands (then see if you can play it with your feet!).

## Half Note and Half Rest

The **Half Note** looks like a quarter note, but with a hole in the dot. A **Half Rest** is a box that sits on the third line.

Draw five Half Notes                    Draw five Half Rests

**HOT TIP:**

Always take a few minutes to fill out the "music writing" exercises. These short drills will help you remember the different types of notes and musical terms.

A half note is equal to TWO quarter notes, so when counting in quarter time, the half note receives TWO counts:

Draw in the **bar lines** to form the notes into **measures.** Check the **time signature** before you begin!

## Single Paradiddle: Step One

The **Single Paradiddle** is the most important rudiment to master because it involves **three** of the five basic strokes required in **all** rudimental drumming. This short exercise isolates the first two strokes of the Paradiddle: the downstroke accent and the soft upstroke.

Count these exercises out loud to a metronome **before** you attempt to play them. After perfecting each line, go back and bounce the 8th notes. Strive for a full, relaxed "buzz" on each hand.

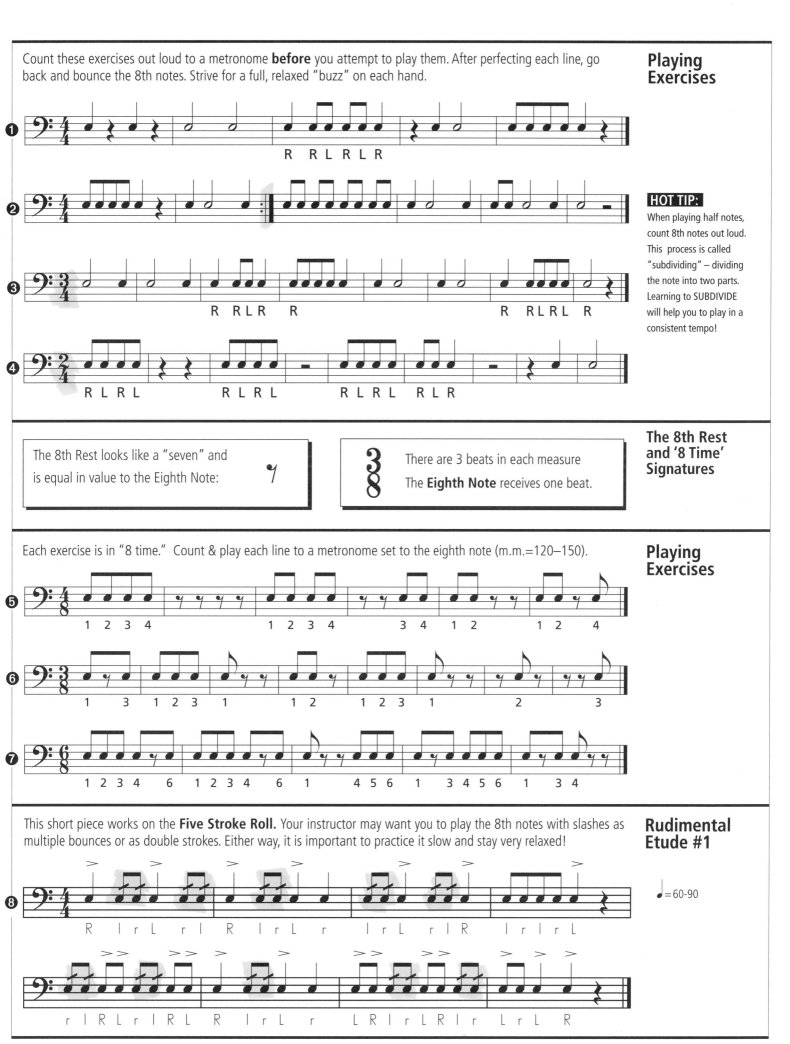

**HOT TIP:**
When playing half notes, count 8th notes out loud. This process is called "subdividing" – dividing the note into two parts. Learning to SUBDIVIDE will help you to play in a consistent tempo!

**The 8th Rest and '8 Time' Signatures**

The 8th Rest looks like a "seven" and is equal in value to the Eighth Note:  ⅞

$\frac{3}{8}$  There are 3 beats in each measure
The **Eighth Note** receives one beat.

**Playing Exercises**

Each exercise is in "8 time." Count & play each line to a metronome set to the eighth note (m.m.=120–150).

**Rudimental Etude #1**

This short piece works on the **Five Stroke Roll.** Your instructor may want you to play the 8th notes with slashes as multiple bounces or as double strokes. Either way, it is important to practice it slow and stay very relaxed!

♩=60-90

# LESSON 5

**Technique WORKOUT**

The fifth and final stroke style to learn is called the **TAP**. Taps are soft, relaxed wrist strokes played at 2-3 inches above the drum. This exercise isolates downstrokes, taps & upstrokes. Practice each hand separately.

Down    tap   tap   tap   tap   up     Down    tap   tap   tap   tap   up
*squeeze*    *RELAX!*        *squeeze*    *RELAX!*

**The Single Paradiddle**

**Step Two**

In step two, you will add the two soft taps that finish the Single Paradiddle.

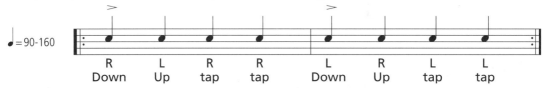

R    L    R    R      L    R    L    L
Down   Up   tap   tap     Down   Up   tap   tap

**Coordination Exercise**

**Homework**

Write the counting under the notes, **then** supply the top number in the time signature.

**8th Rests on the Upbeat**

**HOT TIP:**

Learn each of these lines separately with the PRACTICE tracks before attempting the ACCOMPANIMENT track.

In the following KEY EXERCISES, the 8th **notes** fall on the downbeat, and the 8th **rests** fall on the upbeat. Since the rest is on the upbeat, simply leave out the hand that plays the 'and' or 'te' (the left hand).

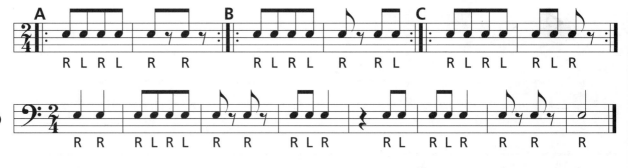

**8th Rests on the Downbeat**

In the next three KEY EXERCISES, the 8th **rests** fall on the downbeats, and the 8th **notes** fall on the upbeats. Since the 8th rest is on the downbeat, simply omit the right hand (and play the upbeat with the left).

These exercises use the 8th rest on the **downbeat**. Follow the stickings and practice with a metronome!

**HOT TIP:**

Since playing upbeat 8th notes is rather difficult, I suggest that you practice for several days on the Lesson 5 Appendix until you get a solid "feel" for the upbeat rhythms.

**HOT TIP:**

Remember to tap your FOOT on each downbeat! Think of "playing your foot" on the downbeat 8th rests in these lines.

The Nine Stroke Roll is four multiple bounces or double strokes, followed by a downstroke.

**The Nine Stroke Roll**

This etude includes some special instructions. The '×' on the top line is played by hitting the sticks together in the air, and the '(⊗)' on the bottom line should be played with **both** sticks on the rim.

**Rudimental Etude #2**

**15**

**Matching:**

Match the correct term with the definition provided.

_____ 1. Music is written on five lines and four spaces. This is called the _____.

_____ 2. A _____ marks the end of a section.

_____ 3. Separates the staff into measures.

_____ 4. Space between two bar lines.

_____ 5. Tells you how fast or slow to play a piece of music.

A. Double Bar

B. Tempo

C. Staff

D. Bar Lines

E. Measure

**Fill in the Blanks:**

Provide the definition for the following time signatures.

$\frac{3}{4}$ _____

$\frac{6}{8}$ _____

**Fill in the Blanks:**

Write the counting under the notes, then give the top number for each time signature.

**Draw in the Bar Lines:**

Separate the notes into measures. Remember to check the time signature before you begin.

**You Draw**

Draw **one** of each of the following:

❶ Quarter Note _____

❷ Half Rest _____

❸ Eighth Rest _____

❹ Half Note _____

❺ Eighth Note _____

❻ Quarter Rest _____

**Technique:**

This is a perfect time to track your progress on the Technique Exercises and Rudiments that you've learned so far. Check the LESSON FIVE progress chart on pages 72 & 78 for a complete list of tempos for each exercise and rudiment.

**At this point in the book, you're ready to start learning to play the drumset!**
**If your teacher doesn't have time to cover the lessons in class,**
**you can also learn ON YOUR OWN with**
**the drumset lessons on page 82 in the back of the book!**

Learn each section of this etude with the PRACTICE tracks (A, B & C) before you attempt to play the entire etude with the ACCOMPANIMENT MP3. Be able to count the rhythms out loud – and play it with the correct sticking!

**Rhythmic Etude**

♩ = 90-120

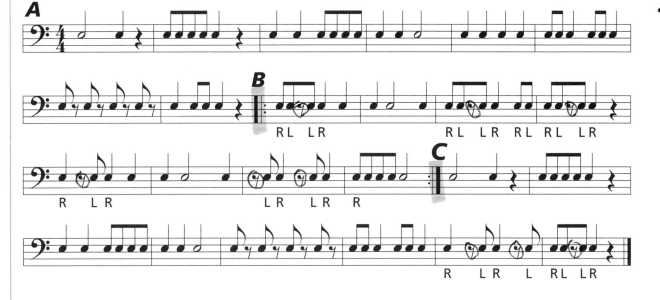

You may wish to play this rudimental etude with multiple bounce rolls or double stroke rolls (or both!). Try to keep a 2-3 inch height on all unaccented notes and use a full stroke (12 inches) for accented notes.

**Rudimental Etude #3**

♩ = 80-100

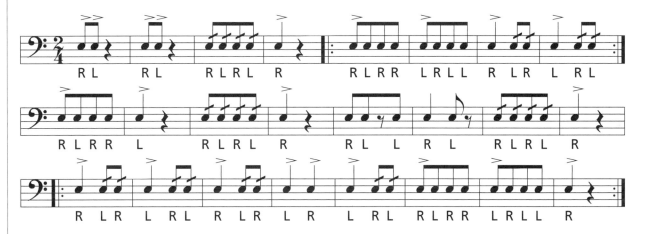

Right hand plays the bottom part on the rim, the left hand plays the top part on the drum head.

**Coordination Etude**

♩ = 90-110

Use an alternating sticking. Practice counting out loud to a metronome before you play.

**Etude in "8 Time"**

♪ = 120-180

# LESSON 6

**Technique WORKOUT**

In this lesson, you'll replace the double stroke exercise #4 with one that works on extended double strokes (#9). You'll also replace exercise #7 with another "two height" exercise (#8). Continue to work on the recommended exercises on the progress chart located on page 72 & 78.

**At least half of each practice session should be spent on technique fundamentals!**

**Sixteenth Notes**

You can recognize the 16th note because it has two flags (remember that the 8th note only has **one** flag). There are **two** 16th notes in each 8th note.

**Homework**

Use the note value chart to fill in the blanks.

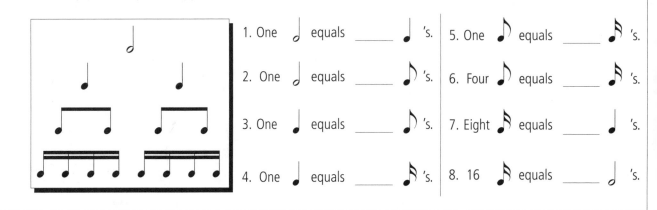

**Key Exercises**

Count each exercise out loud to a metronome before playing them with the practice & accompaniment tracks.

**Playing Exercises**

❶

**HOT TIP:**

Listen for evenness in sound and rhythm while you play the sixteenth notes in these exercises.

❷

❸

18

**HOT TIP:**
DUETS will teach you valuable ensemble skills that you'll need when playing with a full band.

**HOT TIP:**
After you can play each of the lines in this lesson perfectly, go back and play each 16th as a multiple bounce! Try to develop a smooth, consistent "buzz" sound on BOTH hands!

Practice this rudiment as multiple bounce AND double strokes. As we increase the number of bounces in the roll rudiments, count the "skeleton" rhythm or "roll base" out loud while you play.

**The Thirteen Stroke Roll**

♩ = 80-110

Work slowly through this short piece, making sure that the notes **between** the accents (often referred to as **"inner-beats"**) are soft and relaxed, and the accents are strong — with equal volume from both hands.

**Rudimental Etude #4**

♩ = 80-110

# LESSON 7

## Technique WORKOUT:

### The Flam

A **flam** is a combination of a soft tap – called the **grace note** (♪) – and a loud note – the **primary stroke**. Practice several grace notes on each hand. Start with the sticks one inch above the drum. Keep a very relaxed wrist and just "drop" the stick for each grace note, playing each note as soft as possible:

L   L   L   L   L   L   R   R   R   R   R   R

**HOT TIP:**

Listen very carefully to the "sound" of each flam! It's very difficult to get consistent space between the grace note and the primary stroke. Too much space and they will sound like "fa–lam's."

The flam is named for what those two strokes sound like: "faLAM." In this short exercise, you will play three soft grace notes, followed by a full right hand stroke (called the PRIMARY STROKE). As you play the right hand primary stroke, do not LIFT the left hand grace note!

L L L R   L L L R

**Say this while you play:** "fa fa FLAM" "fa fa FLAM"

Once you have the right flam mastered, switch to the opposite hand:

R R R L   R R R L

"fa fa FLAM" "fa fa FLAM"

The Flam is a difficult rudiment to master – and many of the rudiments are built on this important foundation. I highly recommend watching the video lesson on how to play a flam. I also recommend that you take private lessons from a qualified private teacher to learn it correctly!

### Learning to play ALTERNATING FLAMS:

To play alternating flams, play the grace note of the flam as an UP-STROKE and freeze the primary stroke close to the drum. By lifting the grace note and keeping the primary stroke close to the drum, you'll be prepared to play the next flam on the opposite hand!

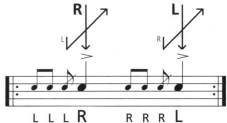

L L L R   R R R L

*Find the video lesson for the flam here:*
www.youtube.com/user/FreshApproachBooks

---

## The Dotted Half Note

A dot behind a note or rest increases its value by **half of the original value** of the note. Since there are two quarters in a half note, a dotted half would be equal to **three** quarters (or three beats in quarter time).

1   2   3   4

This Coordination Exercise utilizes the dotted half note. Play the right hand on the rim and the left hand on the drum.

---

## Exercise for TWO Drums

The note on the second space is for the low–pitched drum and the note on the third space is for the high drum. When playing exercises for more than one drum, always place the highest drum to the right.

R L R   R L R   R L R L R L   R L R   R L R   R L R   R L R L R L

Exercise #4 includes the **one measure repeat sign** (𝄎). When you get to this sign, repeat the **previous** measure.

**Playing Exercises**

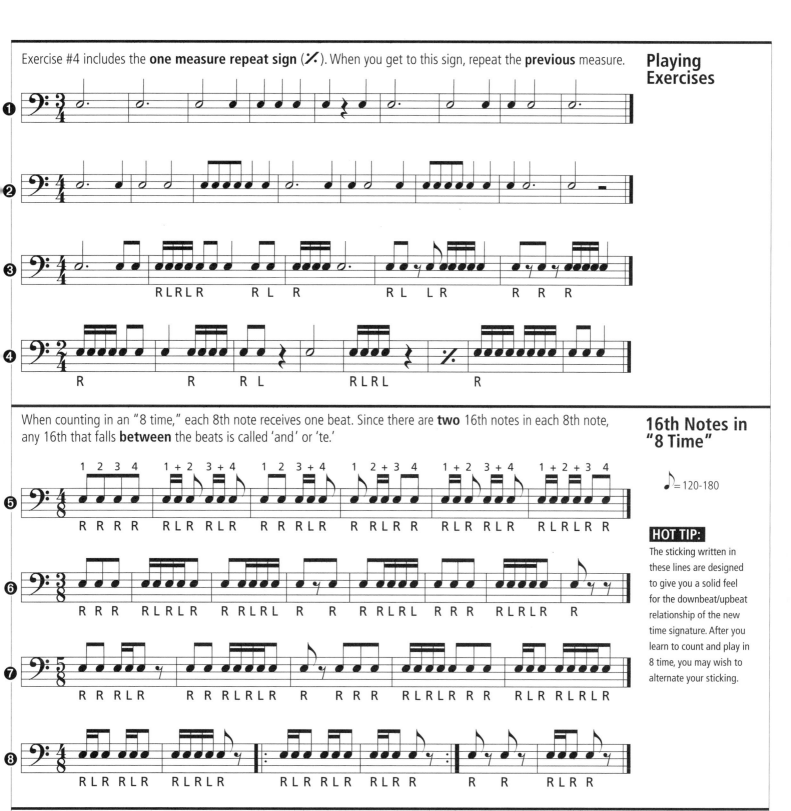

When counting in an "8 time," each 8th note receives one beat. Since there are **two** 16th notes in each 8th note, any 16th that falls **between** the beats is called 'and' or 'te.'

**16th Notes in "8 Time"**

♪ = 120-180

**HOT TIP:**
The sticking written in these lines are designed to give you a solid feel for the downbeat/upbeat relationship of the new time signature. After you learn to count and play in 8 time, you may wish to alternate your sticking.

Play the grace note of each flam as an upstroke so that your hands will be set for the following stroke. Listen carefully to the sound of your flams to develop a consistent spacing between the grace note and primary stroke.

**Rudimental Etude #5**

♩ = 80-110

# LESSON 8

## Technique WORKOUT

Are you spending half of your practice time each day on the Technique Exercises and Rudiments? If you ignore the fundamentals of snare drumming, pretty soon your hands will not be able to play the written music! At this time, you should add the Flam to your daily drill of exercises and rudiments.

## The Whole Note and Whole Rest

THE WHOLE NOTE looks like a half note without the stem and receives **four** beats in quarter time.
The following **Coordination Exercise** uses the whole note.

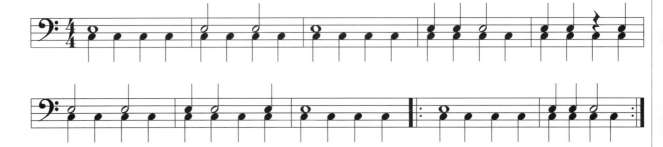

## Homework

A note is missing at the end of each measure. Draw **one note** that corresponds to the missing note. Use the following note values:

## New Rhythm

In this new rhythm, an 8th note takes the place of the last two 16ths:

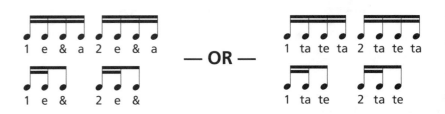

## Key Exercises

Always practice the **correct sticking patterns** while learning new rhythm patterns. Many percussionists cannot play fast rhythmic parts because they are hindered by poor sticking habits.

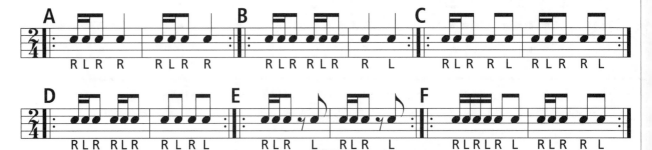

## The Flam Tap

The **Flam Tap** is played with the Alternating Flam, adding a soft tap **between** the flams. Play this rudiment along with the Practice MP3 in Lesson 8 before attempting the Bronze Level rudiment play-along track.

Use the Lesson 8 Appendix in the back of the book for extra practice on this new rhythm.

Playing
Exercises

**HOT TIP:**

The extra lines offered in
the appendix on page 60
will help you develop a
"feel" for new rhythms.
Since they are repetitive,
you can concentrate on
how the hands FEEL when
playing a new rhythm,
rather than having to
concentrate on reading
difficult rhythmic combi-
nations.

The following exercise is a ROUND for two players. The first player begins with the 1st measure. The second player rests for four counts and begins when the first player reaches the second bar.

**Round for
Two Players**

This etude includes the **Flam Tap**. The upstroke motion of the flams should be exactly the same in measure 1 and measure 2. Work to achieve a consistent sound on each flam — keeping the grace note low and relaxed.

**Rudimental
Etude #6**

♩ = 100-130

# LESSON 9

**Technique WORKOUT:**

**Single Stroke Seven**

The Single Stroke Seven is a new RUDIMENT that will increase your speed on rebound strokes. It is played exactly as the name implies: with seven single strokes! First "vocalize" it, then play it several times starting on each hand:

| Say this: | "DIG | a | da | dig | a | da | DAH" |
|---|---|---|---|---|---|---|---|
| Play this: | R | L | R | L | R | L | R |
| or this: | L | R | L | R | L | R | L |

---

**New Rhythm**

In this new rhythm, an 8th note takes the place of the first two 16ths:

–OR–

---

**Key Exercises**

Count each exercise out loud before you play. Watch the sticking provided.

---

**Duet**

This duet is two lines long. Practice each part separately with a metronome before playing together.

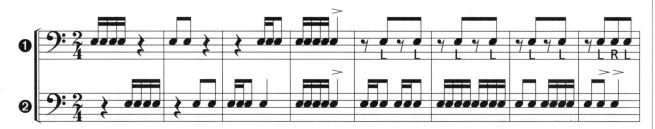

**HOT TIP:**

Duets make great "ensemble" practice. If you don't have a friend to play along with, try playing the opposite part with the PRACTICE playalong tracks.

---

**The Flam Paradiddle**

**Step One**

♩=60-120

In exercise #1, practice playing a right hand flam, **but do not play the grace note as an upstroke**. The grace note **must** remain low because the second stroke of the Flam Paradiddle is played as an upstroke (exercise #2).

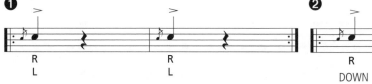

Watch the sticking **very carefully!** Work with a metronome whenever possible.

# Playing Exercises

**HOT TIP:**
After you get a line worked up, go back through and play a multiple bounce on every 16th. If you've been practicing your multiple bounce, then you should hear a smooth "buzz roll" on each 16th note pattern.

# Two Drum Etude

Start this exercise very slowly and strive to use a smooth arm motion when moving from drum to drum.

Try to **relax** the hands on the strokes between the accents. It is important to control the rebound of the stick on the accented downstrokes (to freeze the stick close to the drum), but remember to relax on the innerbeats!

# Rudimental Etude #7

Listen closely to the sound of each FLAM while you play. Do not allow the hands to hit at the same time!

**25**

# LESSON 10

**Technique WORKOUT**

This new exercise works on the three 16th note rhythmic patterns that you've learned so far. To test your "timing," try playing it as a ROUND with 2 or more players!

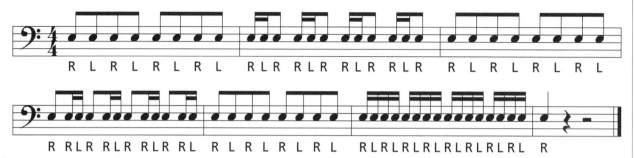

R L R L R L R L     R L R R L R R L R R L R     R L R L R L R L

R R L R R L R R L R R L     R L R L R L R L     R L R L R L R L R L R L R L R L     R

**Duet**

This duet is three lines long and includes some special instructions. The '×' on the top line should be played with alternating strokes on the rim, and the '⊗' on the 2nd line should be played by hitting the sticks together in the air.

**HOT TIP:**

Listen carefully to the other player as you play duets or ensembles! Not only should you concentrate on playing together, but you should also make sure that you are matching volume levels.

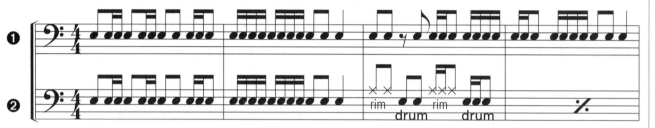

rim  rim
drum  drum

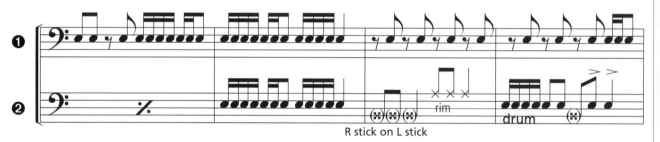

R stick on L stick

(⊗)(⊗)(⊗)  rim
drum  (⊗)

(⊗)(⊗)(⊗)  × × ×  (⊗)

**The Dotted Quarter Note**

Remember that a dot placed behind a note or rest **increases its value by half** of its original value. Since there are two 8th notes in a quarter, a **dotted quarter note** would be equal to **three** 8th notes:

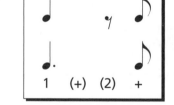

1  (+)  (2)  +

If ♩ = ♫ then ♩. = ♫ + ♪

**A**          **B**          **C**

R   L   R   L   R   L   R   L     R   L   R   L     R   L   R   L   R

**D**          **E**          **F**

R L R L R L R   R L R L R L R     R R L R L R L   R R L R L R L     R   R L R L R   R   R L R L R

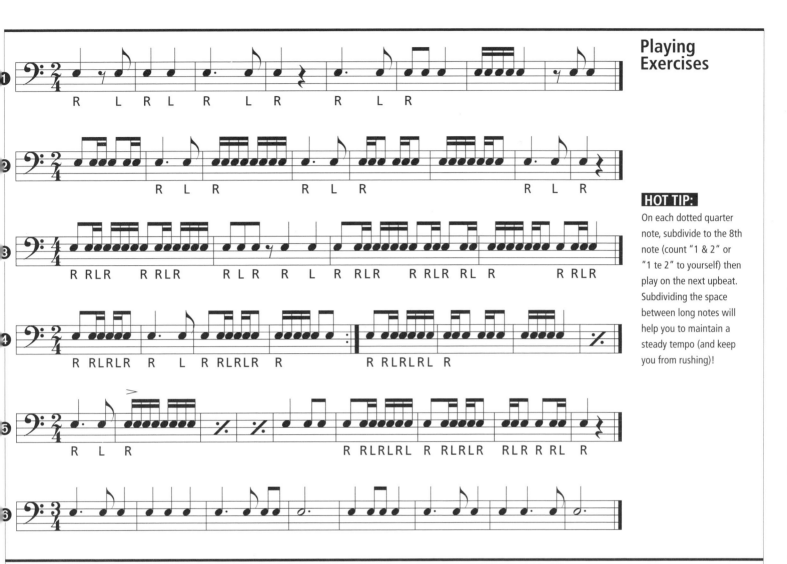

**HOT TIP:**

On each dotted quarter note, subdivide to the 8th note (count "1 & 2" or "1 te 2" to yourself) then play on the next upbeat. Subdividing the space between long notes will help you to maintain a steady tempo (and keep you from rushing)!

## The Flam Paradiddle

**Step Two**

**HOT TIP:**

Be sure to watch the YouTube lesson video for this important rudiment! The fundamentals you'll learn now will apply to many of the other flam rudiments!

In this exercise, we add the remaining two taps that finish the **Flam Paradiddle**. The primary stroke of each flam should be played at 12 inches (a full stroke), and the innerbeats and grace notes should be soft and relaxed at 2–3 inches. Listen to the sound of each "fLAM" to make sure you're not playing "POP's!"

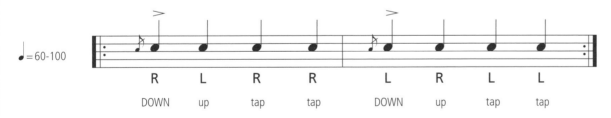

Each stroke of the Flam Paradiddle must be **perfected** before moving on to the Rudimental Etude.

## Rudimental Etude #8

Say the sticking of the Flam Paradiddle out loud as you play this etude and listen to the sound of each of the flams!

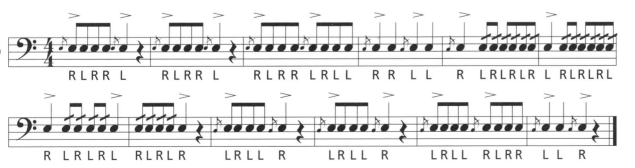

**You Draw**

Supply the missing note in the following measures. Use only **one note** in each measure from the following note values:

**Fill in the Blanks!**

Write in the counting under the notes, **then** give the top number in the time signatures.

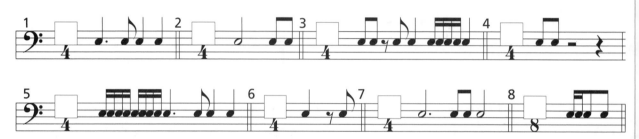

**Technique Workout**

To make sure that your technical development is on par with your rhythm reading development, check to see if you can play each exercise and rudiment at the recommended tempos for the LESSON TEN progress chart on page 72 & 78.

Of course, speed should not be the only consideration when practicing the Technique Exercises and Rudiments! Proper attention to the correct stroke styles and evenness of sound is most important. You will only be able to achieve speed if you're practicing the correct stroke styles at a slow tempo first!

If you haven't started to learn to play the DRUMSET by this point in the book, I highly encourage you to do so! To become a well rounded percussionist, you'll eventually be asked to play drumset parts – even if you're only going to play in the school band.

The DRUMSET FUNDAMENTALS section in the appendix on page 82 will take you step-by step through all of the essential skills! Even if you don't own a drumset and learn by playing with your hands on your legs, you'll have fun playing the grooves along with some great tunes!

**Etude in "8 time"**

Start slowly, gradually working up the tempo marked.

♪ = 160

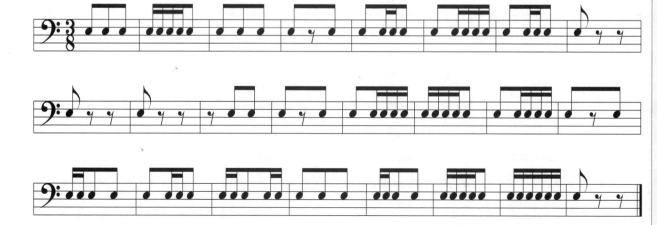

## Rhythmic Etude

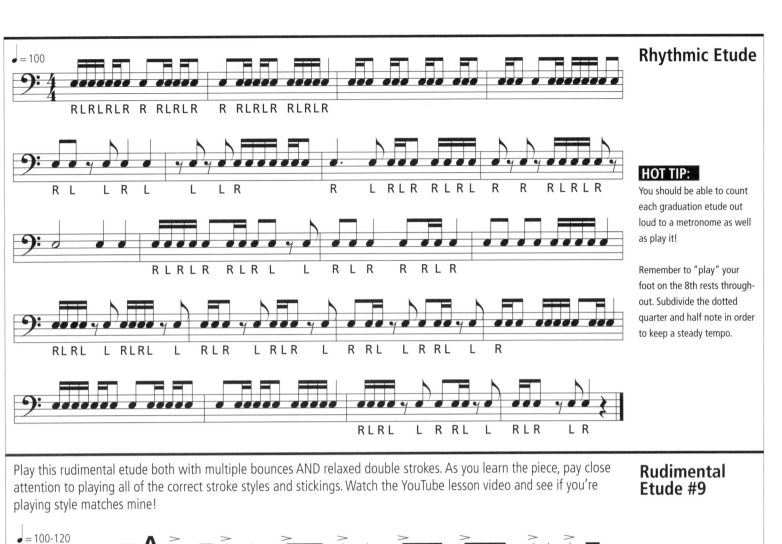

**HOT TIP:**

You should be able to count each graduation etude out loud to a metronome as well as play it!

Remember to "play" your foot on the 8th rests throughout. Subdivide the dotted quarter and half note in order to keep a steady tempo.

## Rudimental Etude #9

Play this rudimental etude both with multiple bounces AND relaxed double strokes. As you learn the piece, pay close attention to playing all of the correct stroke styles and stickings. Watch the YouTube lesson video and see if you're playing style matches mine!

**HOT TIP:**

Stay as relaxed as possible on the innerbeats and rolls! Speed and consistency will only develop if you have a smooth, relaxed approach to the snare drum.

## Two Drum Etude

Most of the paradiddles in the following etude are played **without** accents. Strive to achieve a smooth, even sound when playing the 16th notes drum to drum.

# LESSON 11

## Technique WORKOUT:

## Double Bounce

So far, we've been working on exercises that utilize relaxed double STROKES. At this point, it is important to learn to turn the relaxed double wrist stroke into a double BOUNCE.

A double bounce is similar to the multiple bounce except that it is produced with a relaxed fulcrum. The squeeze on the fulcrum "regulates" the space between the bounced notes. Start with 4 relaxed wrist strokes in the first measure, then squeeze the fulcrum just enough to produce a double bounce on each wrist turn in the second measure:

**HOT TIP:**

Avoid squeezing the sticks with the back fingers. The fingers should be touching the stick lightly, but without choking the bounce of the stick!

Once you're able to play relaxed double bounces on the right and left separately, try this next exercise. Keep the wrist motion the same from measure one to measure two and adjust the squeeze on the fulcrum in order to produce even sounding bounces:

Download practice MP3's for each line in Lesson11 through the end of the book on my website:
**http://www.mwpublications.com/category/educational-content/**

## Quarter Note Rolls

Rolls are usually notated with "slashes" through the stem of a note. A single slash through the 16th notes tells you to bounce each note. THREE slashes through a note tells you to "roll" for the length of that particular note. For now, we will play rolls by bouncing 16th notes.

Since a quarter note equals four 16th notes, a quarter note roll is **four 16ths bounced.** Count each quarter note roll as you would four 16ths:

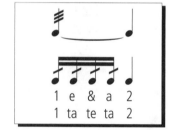

Keep the wrist motion consistent in each one of the rolls in these KEY EXERCISES:

## Playing Exercises

Alternate between multiple bounce (buzz) rolls and double bounce rolls in the following exercises.

**HOT TIP:**

Always count the 16th note "base rhythm" of the quarter note rolls ('1 e & a' or '1 ta te ta'). Being able to count the "roll base" or "roll skeleton" will help you to develop consistent sound and evenness on your rolls.

## Playing Exercises, Continued

Count the quarter note rolls in the following exercises in "8 time" as you would four 16th notes.

## Quarter Note Rolls in "8 Tme"

Use the sticking provided for you until you get comfortable with the time signatures.

**HOT TIP:**

It is important to develop "open rolls" AND "buzz rolls." Practice each one of these lines first with one, then the other.

The **Double Paradiddle** adds an accent and a tap to the beginning of the Single Paradiddle. Practice the "single accent" double paradiddle as well (leaving out the 2nd accent).

## The Double Paradiddle

At the slowest tempo marked, play double STROKES on each roll. Once you speed up, relax the fulcrum and play double BOUNCES.

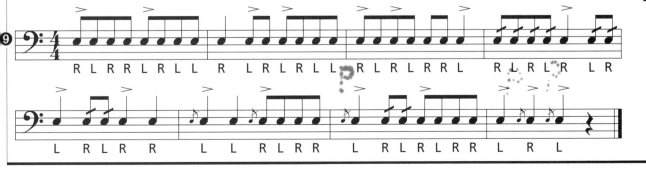

## Rudimental Etude #10

♩ = 100-150

31

# LESSON 12

**Technique WORKOUT:**

This new technique exercise isolates double bounce strokes (sometimes called "diddles"). At the slowest tempo, work to play 2 relaxed WRIST strokes on each diddle. As you speed up, turn the diddle into a double BOUNCE.

**Double Strokes**

♩ = 100-130

**Double Bounces**

♩ = 140-160

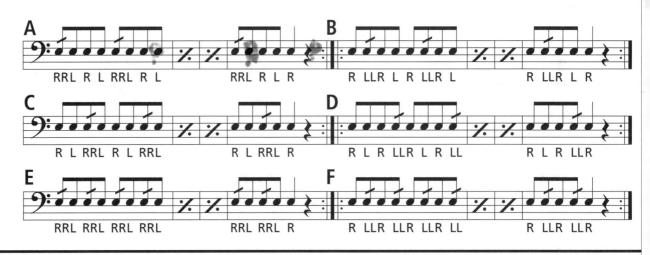

**Coordination Exercises**

In "8 Time." Start at the slowest tempo marked, then gradually increase the speed.

**The Half Note Roll**

Since a half note equals **eight** 16th notes, a half note roll is eight 16th notes bounced. Count each half note roll as you would eight 16ths.

Count the 16th note "roll base" for each of the rolls in these Playing Exercises.

**HOT TIP:**

Practice on a snare drum as much as possible! Practice pads can approximate the feel of a real drum, but being able to hear the sound of your rolls on a drum is also very important!

## Playing Exercises, Continued

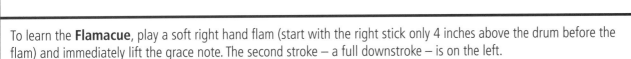

## Review: Quarter Rolls in "8 Time"

## The Flamacue
### Step One

♩ = 100-180

To learn the **Flamacue**, play a soft right hand flam (start with the right stick only 4 inches above the drum before the flam) and immediately lift the grace note. The second stroke – a full downstroke – is on the left.

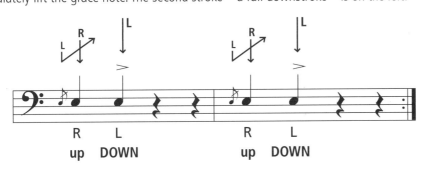

## Rudimental Etude #11

♩ = 90-130

Start at the slowest tempo marked and work to achieve a 2–3 inch height on all grace notes and inner beats.

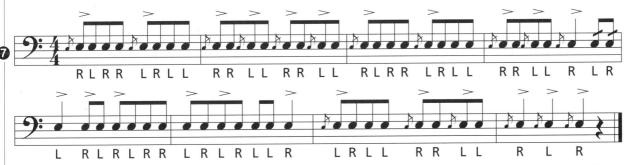

# LESSON 13

**Technique WORKOUT**

This exercise helps with the alternating flam by working on accent and grace note heights. The 2 height motion in the first measure should be exactly the same as you play the flams in the second measure.

R R R R R R R R  R L R L R L R  L L L L L L L L  L R L R L R L

---

**Dynamic Markings**

**Dynamic Markings** are used in music to tell us how loud or soft to play. The three most common dynamic markings listed here are used in the following duet.

| | | | |
|---|---|---|---|
| $f$ | : | **FORTE** | : | Loud |
| $mf$ | : | **MEZZO FORTE** | : | Medium Loud |
| $p$ | : | **PIANO** | : | Soft |

**HOT TIP:**

Composers often use dynamics to create musical effects. The piano volume level in this duet is used to create an "accompaniment" part while the stronger voice has the "melody" – or lead line.

---

**8th Note Rolls: On the Downbeat**

Since there are only **two** 16th notes in a 8th note, an 8th note roll is **two** 16ths bounced. When beating time to the quarter, an 8th note roll on the downbeat is counted "1–e–&" or "1–ta–te."

A    RLR R    R R R    B    RLR R R  RLR R  R    C    RLRLR R  R  RLR R

**HOT TIP:**

Strive to achieve a consistent volume level between your rolls and surrounding notes. Each flam should have consistent 1 inch heights on the grace notes.

---

**34**

8th note rolls on the upbeat are counted "1  &-a-2" or "1  te-ta-2." Follow the sticking in these exercises.

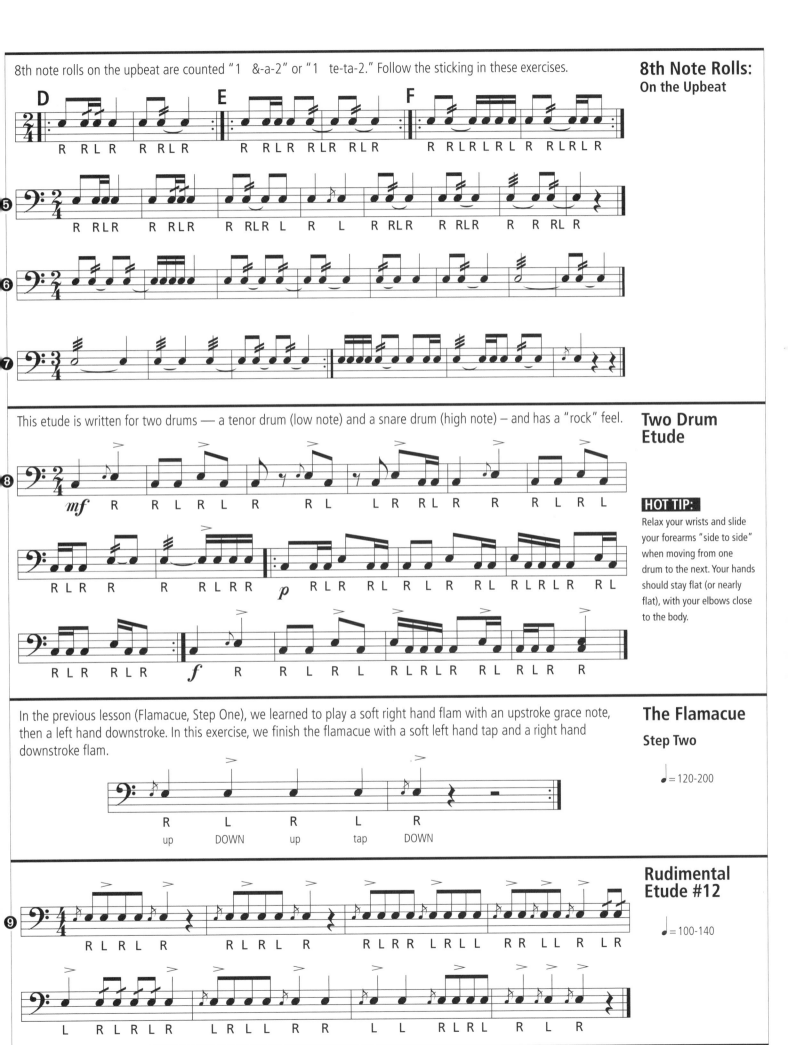

This etude is written for two drums — a tenor drum (low note) and a snare drum (high note) – and has a "rock" feel.

**Two Drum Etude**

**HOT TIP:**
Relax your wrists and slide your forearms "side to side" when moving from one drum to the next. Your hands should stay flat (or nearly flat), with your elbows close to the body.

In the previous lesson (Flamacue, Step One), we learned to play a soft right hand flam with an upstroke grace note, then a left hand downstroke. In this exercise, we finish the flamacue with a soft left hand tap and a right hand downstroke flam.

**The Flamacue**

**Step Two**

♩ = 120-200

**Rudimental Etude #12**

♩ = 100-140

**35**

# LESSON 14

**Technique WORKOUT**

The progress chart on page 72 & 78 has a complete list of exercises and rudiments that you should be working on at this point in the book. Because the list grows as you add more techniques and rudiments, you might need to alternate between them (select a couple rudiments from each family rather than work on all of them in one practice session).

**Developing great technique requires mental discipline and consistent practice!**

## More Dynamic Markings

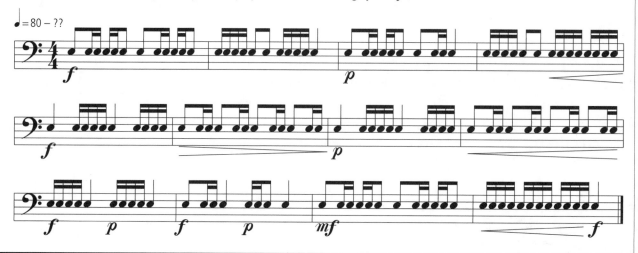

: **Crescendo** : Gradually get louder

: **Diminuendo** : Gradually get softer

This short piece uses all of the dynamic markings that we have learned so far. Start at the slowest tempo marked, then work up to the fastest tempo that you can play (without sacrificing **quality!**).

**HOT TIP:**

Avoid the "age–old" problem that most drummers have: rushing when you play louder! Work with a metronome to develop tempo control on all dynamic levels!

## New Rhythm

Notice that in this new rhythm, the 8th **rest** takes the place of the first 8th **note**.

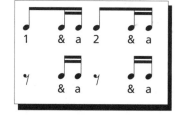 –OR–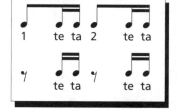

Keep the back fingers in contact with the stick when playing rolls. Also, make sure that you are not "pulsating" your right hand (playing the right hand stronger than the left).

**HOT TIP:**

Count the first two 16ths out loud on the 8th rest in this new rhythm pattern. SUBDIVIDING a rest will keep you from rushing and also help rhythmic accuracy.

## New Rhythm

Notice that in this new rhythm, the 8th rest falls on the **upbeat**.

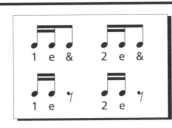

–OR–

## Reviewing Rolls in "8 Time"

Remember to count each quarter note roll as you would four 16th notes. Practice both types of rolls: open (double bounce) rolls and buzz (multiple bounce) rolls.

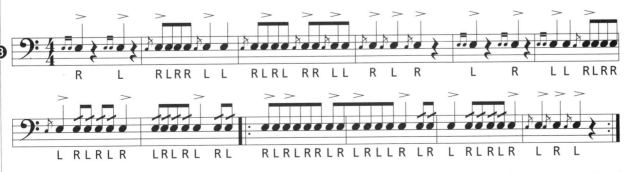

## The Alternating Drag

$\quad$ = 100-140

Like the flam, the **drag** is a combination of an upstroke (this time bounced), and a downstroke. Unlike the flam however, a drag is played with a "pickup" bounce stroke, with more space before the primary stroke. Practice the long buzz "pickup strokes" in Exercise A for several days before attempting the double bounce drag in Exercise B.

**A**

**B**

## Rudimental Etude #13

$\quad$ = 100-140

Make sure that you "prep" the stick heights for each one of the drags in this etude (set the hands at grace note/accent note heights). Think of each drag as two separate strokes (and-ONE, and-TWO) until you get the feel for it.

37

# LESSON 15

## Technique WORKOUT

♪ = 120-240

Each of these short exercises work on playing accent patterns in 6/8. Make sure that you are playing with only "two heights" – a full stroke height (12 inches) on the accents and the soft tap height (2-3 inches) on the "innerbeats." Once you have them all perfected, learn Exercise #17 in the back of the book.

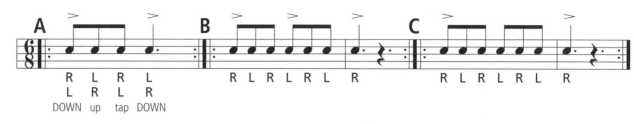

DOWN up tap DOWN

## New Musical Terms

| | | |
|---|---|---|
| **poco a poco** | : | little by little -or- gradually |
| **ritardando (abbr. ritard)** | : | gradually slacking in speed |
| **fine (pronounced FEE-nay)** | : | the end or close: the finish |
| **fermata (⌢)** | : | hold or pause |

This etude incorporates the new musical terms. The last line even combines some of the terms to tell you how to play the entire line! The dotted half note roll in this etude is equal in value to **three counts** of bounced 16th notes.

**HOT TIP:**

On the MP3, you'll notice that I use the buzz roll. Listen closely to the sound of each roll! If you are working consistently on the sound of your buzz strokes, you will be able to make your rolls sound just as good!

## The Drag Paradiddle #2

The Drag Paradiddle #2 is a combination of two drags and a Single Paradiddle.

The 'slash' notation in this first example literally means to play two strokes in the place of each 8th note (two 16th notes), so if you are playing in a slow tempo, the double will be very open – just as you would play 16ths.

R LL R LL R L R R    L RR L RR L R L L

This example utilizes the "traditional" way of notating the drags. In this example, the drag always sounds the same – no matter the tempo. A good percussionist should be able to play drags with either interpretation.

R LL R LL R L R R    L RR L RR L R L L

The whole note roll in Exercise #3 is equal in value to **4 counts** of bounced 16th notes.

**Pick–Up Notes** begin **before** the first measure and are borrowed from the last measure.

**Pick–Up Notes**

**HOT TIP:**

You have to use your "music math" skills to determine where to play pickup notes.

Count the 8th note rolls in the following exercises as you would two sixteenths: "1-&-2" or "1-te-2." Notice that in exercise #6, the first two measures are counted exactly alike.

**Eighth Note
Rolls in "8 Time"**

Play the Drags and Drag Paradiddles with the "traditional" interpretation in this rudimental etude.

**Rudimental
Etude #14**

**HOT TIP:**

In "rudimental" style drumming, rolls always have a consistent interpretation – play them as exact subdivisions of the roll base.

## Fill in the Blanks

Provide the definition for the following musical terms and symbols.

❶ $f$ _____

❷ ⌢ _____

❸ ◁ _____

❹ $mf$ _____

❺ ▷ _____

❻ poco a poco _____

❼ ritardando _____

❽ $p$ _____

❾ fine _____

❿ 𝄍 _____

## You Draw

Supply the missing note in the following measures. Use only **one note from the following note values:**

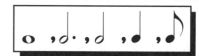

## Technique WORKOUT

To make sure that your technical development is on par with your rhythm reading development, check to see if you can play each exercise and rudiment at the recommended tempos for the LESSON FIFTEEN progress chart on page 72 & 78.

Of course, speed should not be the only consideration when practicing the Technique Exercises and Rudiments! Proper attention to the correct stroke styles and evenness of sound is most important. You will only be able to achieve speed if you're practicing the correct stroke styles at a slow tempo first!

> This is a good time to also learn the other Paradiddle rudiments (the Triple Paradiddle and Paradiddle-diddle), plus the Drag Paradiddle #1. Since you've established a solid foundation, learning new rudiments should be easy!

## Two Drum Etude

Including the Single and Double Paradiddle. Start slow, with 6 beats to a measure. Watch the stickings!

 = 140-180

Try to make the dynamics consistent throughout this etude (the piano should always have the same volume, no matter where you are in the etude).

Notice that is etude includes a repeated section with different dynamic levels. The first time through, play **piano**, the second time, play **forte**. Use buzz rolls on this etude.

**Rhythmic Etude: In "8 Time"**

♪=140-180

Use "open" rolls in the Rudimental Etudes. Strive for a clean double bounce on each roll and drag.

**Rudimental Etude #15**

♩=120-150

**41**

# LESSON 16

**Technique WORKOUT**

This new exercise works on accented flam patterns. Perfect the accented pattern in the first measure, then add the flam in the second. Add this exercise (#18 on page 76) to the recommended progress list of exercises and rudiments.

RLRLRL    RLRLRLRL    RLRLRLRL    RLRLRLRL

**Music Math**

Add the note values together to find a total number of counts **in quarter time**.

❶ 1 ♩ + 1 ♩ + 1 𝅝 = _____ counts.

❷ 2 ♩ + 1 ♩ + 2 ♪ = _____ counts.

❸ 2 𝅝 + 3 𝄽 + 1 ♩. = _____ counts.

❹ 2 ♪ + 1 ▬ + 1 ♩ = _____ counts.

❺ 2 𝄽 + 1 ▬ + 4 ♪ = _____ counts.

❻ 2 ♪ + 4 ♪ + 1 ♩. = _____ counts.

**Coordination Exercise**

Percussionists are often called upon to play drumset parts in band music. Here's a few exercises to work simple hi-hat, snare combinations. If you have a drumset, try playing the bass drum on all four beats.

A    R L R R    R L R R
B    R L R R
C    R L R R

**The Sixteenth Rest**

The **sixteenth rest** has two "flags" and looks similar to the 8th rest (which has **one** flag). The 16th rest in this new rhythm takes the place of the first 16th note:

 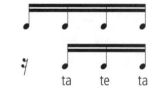

e    &    a    –OR–    ta    te    ta

**HOT TIP:**
Think of "playing your foot" on each 16th rest on this new rhythm and follow the sticking carefully!

A    R L R L R  L    L R L R  L
B    R L R L R    L R L R
C    L R L R L R    L R L R  L

D    R L R L    L R L  R
E    R L R L    L R L R  L
F    L R L R  L    R

**Playing Exercises**

❶

R L R L R  L    L R L R  L    L R L R    R L R L    L R L R    L R L R

**HOT TIP:**
Work with a metronome to ensure the rhythmic accuracy of the left hand entrance after the 16th rest.

❷

R  R L R  L    L R L R    R  L    L R L R L R

❸

L R L R L R    L R L R    R  L    R L R L    L R L    R L    R

Exercise #4 is a **musical** study that applies all of the rhythms and dynamics that you have encountered in the book.

## Musical Study for Snare Drum

♩= 90-110

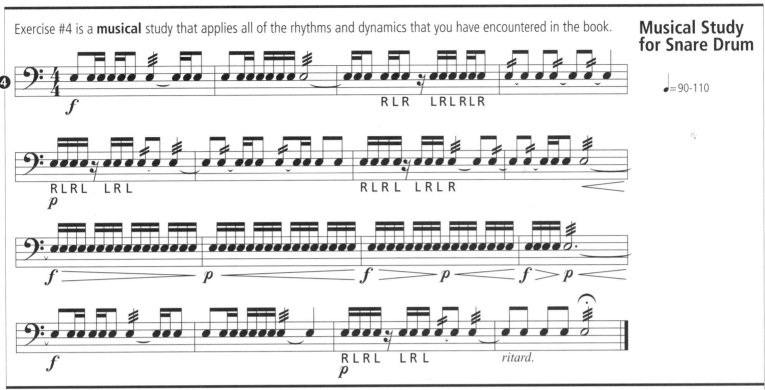

The seven stroke roll uses the new rhythm that you have learned, only bouncing the 16th notes. This new rudiment can also be played with an accent added to the beginning (Exercise B & C). Since this added stroke is not bounced, this version of the seven stroke roll is often called a **tap roll**.

## The Seven Stroke Roll

A composer will often designate a different ending to be played on the repeat of a musical phrase. This is indicated by **first and second ending signs.**

## First & Second Endings

In this example, play measure 1 and 2, the first ending (meas. 3), then repeat back to the beginning. Play measure 1 and 2 again, SKIP the 1st ending (meas. 3), and finish with the second ending (measure 4).

## Rudimental Etude #16

### HOT TIP:

Sometimes a flam at the beginning of a 7 stroke roll will cause a tempo problem. Practice count two of measure 4 until you are able to keep an even 16th note base.

# LESSON 17

**Technique WORKOUT**

On this lesson, you will replace the "Chicken and a Roll" exercise with one that adds TAP ROLLS (#19). Check the progress chart on page 72 & 78 during each practice session to see your progress on the Technique Exercises and rudiments. Sometimes it's a good idea to go back to an old exercise to brush up on it as well!

**Homework**

A note is missing in the following measures. Draw only **one note to complete each measure.**

**New Rhythm**

In this new rhythm, the 16th rest falls on the third 16th note. Notice that this rhythm can be written two ways:

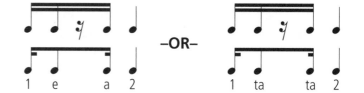

1 e a 2   –OR–   1 ta ta 2

**Playing Exercises**

**The Lesson 25**

Make sure that the bounced 16th note and two taps following the accent are played **soft** and **relaxed!** Work on both interpretations.

This trio is written for snare drum, cymbals and bass drum and can be used for a "street beat" or drum cadence at football games, pep rallies or parades.

The techniques for playing bass drum and cymbals are covered on page 70.

The techniques for playing bass drum and cymbals are covered on page 70.

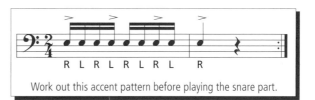

Work out this accent pattern before playing the snare part.

## Drum Cadence

**A**

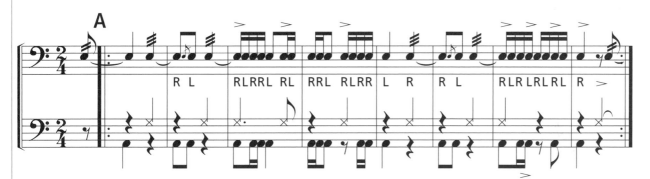

**B**

**HOT TIP:**

In order to play a difficult ensemble, the players must first be able to play their individual parts perfectly with a metronome! Most ensemble "problems" occur when one player has difficulty keeping a rhythm in tempo.

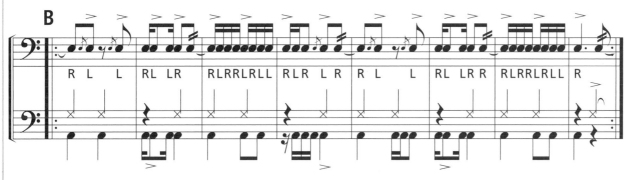

**C**

stick clicks

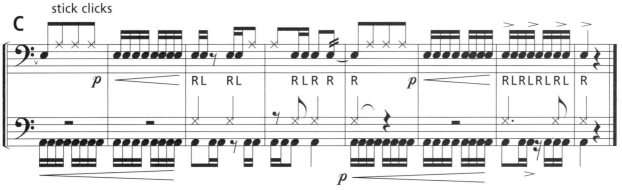

The Lesson 25 in this etude is written with the "modern" interpretation. As you alternate back and forth between the Lesson 25 and the Seven Stroke Roll in the second line, keep a consistent hand motion.

## Rudimental Etude #17

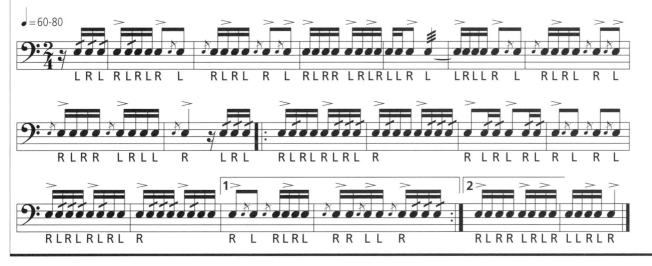

# LESSON 18

**Technique WORKOUT**

As speed increases on Flam Taps, it becomes necessary to play rebound strokes instead of controlled strokes. Use a full stroke on the accent, but allow the stick to rebound for the second and third notes. Repeat on the opposite hand.

RRR RRR RRR RRR    RRR RRR RRR RRR    RR L RR L RR L RR L

**Dotted Eighth Notes**

Remember that a dot behind a note INCREASES ITS VALUE BY HALF of its original value. Since one 8th note equals **two** 16ths, a **dotted eighth note** would be equal to **three** 16ths:

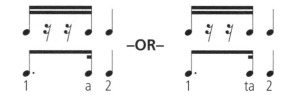

**HOT TIP:**

Subdivide every dotted 8th note by counting the first three 16ths. This will help keep an even spacing on this new rhythm pattern.

A    R L R L R    R    L R    B    R    L R    R    L R    C    R    L R L R    L R L

D    R    L R L R L    R    L R L R L    E    R    L R    R    L R    F    R    L R    L R L R

**Playing Exercises**

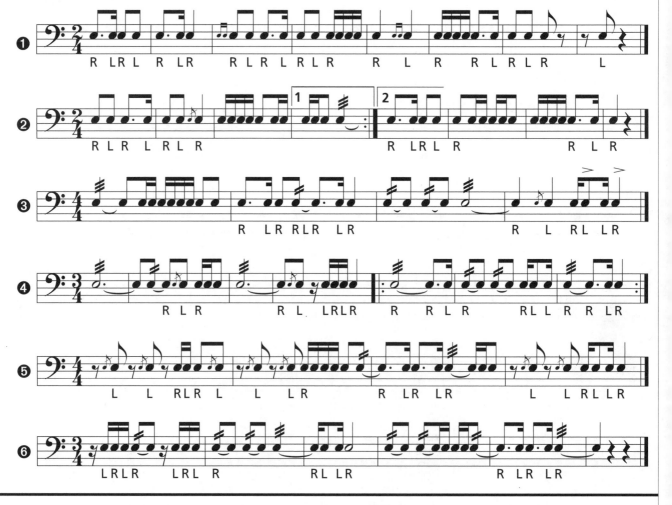

❶   R L R L   R   L R    R L R L R L R    R   L   R   R L R L R    L

❷   R L R   L R L R    **1**   **2** R   L R L R    R L R

❸   R   L R R L R   L R    R   L   R L   L R

❹   R L R    R L   L R L R    R   R L R    R L L R R L R

❺   L   L   R L R L   L   L R    R   L R   L R    L   L R L L R

❻   L R L R   L R L   R    R L   L R    R   L R   L R

**The Single Drag**

All "drag" and roll rudiments should be played with **double bounces.** "Squeeze" slightly on the accents, but remember to relax the fulcrum on the innerbeats.

A   R L L R   L R R L    B   R   L L R   L   R R L

Spend a few minutes to memorize these new musical terms.

**New Musical Terms**

| **Accelerando** | **Fine** | **D.C. al Fine** |
|---|---|---|
| abbreviated "accel." | pronounced "fee-nay" | "Da Cah-poe aul fee-nay" |
| gradually get faster | the finish — the end | Go back to the beginning and play to the finish. |

**Etude for Low Tom, Snare and Suspended Cymbal**

The low tom-tom (notated on the 1st space) should be placed on the left, the snare in the middle, and the suspended cymbal to the right.

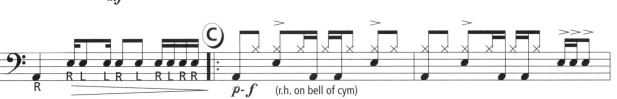

**HOT TIP:**

Work out the rhythms, stickings and dynamics at a VERY slow tempo before you attempt to play it as fast as I do on the MP3! Set your metronome on a slow tempo and be able to play a section PERFECTLY FOUR TIMES IN A ROW before you try it faster. If you practice making mistakes, you'll perform with mistakes!

**Rudimental Etude #18**

Try to play REBOUND strokes on the Flam Taps in this etude. Since the stick is allowed to rebound, you will hear a difference in sound between regular downstroke accents (sometimes called "staccato strokes") and rebound accents (sometimes called "legato strokes").

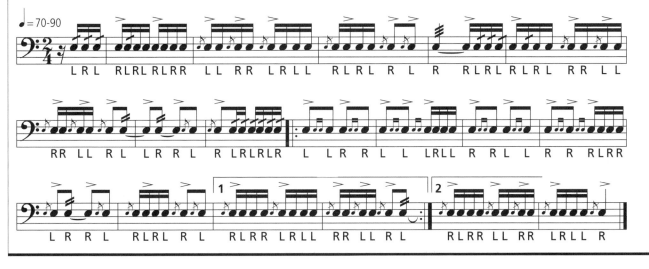

# LESSON 19

**Technique WORKOUT**

On this exercise, you'll add exercise #21 (which works on Flam Accents and Single Drags) and #22 (which adds the "triplet" version of the 5 stroke roll). First work your way through the Flam Accent exercises on the bottom of this page to learn the concept, then add #21 and #22 to your daily practice routine. Being able to play the techniques and rudiments is very important if you want to be able to play "The Finish Line" at the end of the book!

**Eighth Note Triplets**

A **triplet** is a grouping of three notes. The three notes of a triplet are equal to TWO notes of the same value.

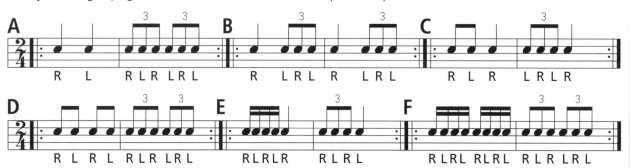

**Playing Exercises**

Make sure that the triplet is evenly spaced through the beat. Practice with a metronome to ensure accuracy.

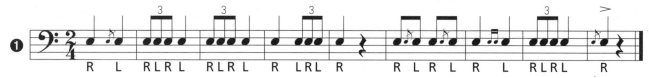

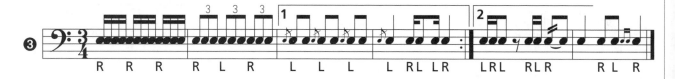

**Review of "8 Time"**

**The Flam Accent**

The **Flam Accent** is played just like the Flam Paradiddle, minus one tap (a downstroke flam, an upstroke, and one tap). The Flam Accent is typically written with an 8th note triplet (ex. A & B), but can also be written in quarter time (ex. C).

A **CODA** is a special ending placed on a piece of music. In the snare etude below, play through to the **D.C.** (Da Capo), then repeat back to the beginning. Play until you see the **Coda sign**: then jump to the new ending (the **Coda**).

**Etude for Snare Drum:** This short piece includes **meter changes**. Notice that you will beat time to the quarter note throughout, so the only change between $^4/_4$, $^3/_4$ and $^2/_4$ is the **number of beats per measure**.

**HOT TIP:**
Whenever you play "concert" style snare drum solos or etudes, you should use buzz rolls. In this style, you should also play "closed" or "buzzed" grace notes on each ruff to match the musical style of the buzz rolls. Listen carefully to the style of the rolls and ruffs on the MP3.

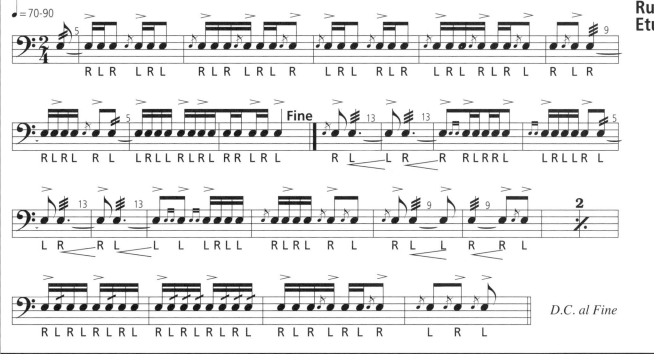

**Rudimental Etude #19**

D.C. al Fine

49

# LESSON 20

**Technique WORKOUT**

Congratulations! You've made it to the FINAL LESSON in the book! To finish out your technique training, add Technique Exercise #23 to the list of exercises that you work on each day. You'll probably notice right away that the exercise utilizes the Single Stroke 4 and the Single Stroke 7. If you've been working consistently on these rudiments, this exercise will be a breeze!

**Cut Time**

In "Cut Time," the player beats time to the **half note**. Half notes fall on the downbeats, quarters fall on the upbeats, etc. Count these Key Exercises out loud to a metronome before you play.

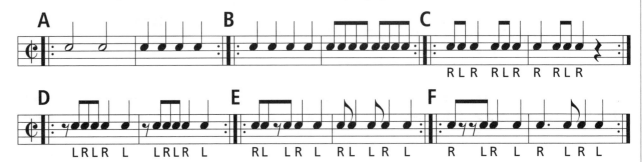

**Rolls in Cut Time**

In Cut Time, rolls are counted like 16th notes **in quarter time**. In order to play rolls in cut time, you must now bounce the 8th note!

**Playing Exercises**

Go back through Lessons 4 – 15 and play the Rudimental Etudes while beating time to the half note.

**Musical Term: Dal Segno**

When a composer wishes you to repeat a portion of a piece of music, he or she may use a **Dal Segno** repeat — usually is indicated with a **D.S.** (see the snare etude at the top of the next page). When you reach the Dal Segno (or D.S.), repeat back to this sign:

A Tie is an arching line connecting two notes of the same pitch — indicating that the 2nd note should not be played, but should be added in value to the first.

**Ties**

This etude uses a technique that you see often in jazz or pop music. The weak beats (upbeats or the "e's & a's") are accented, causing a swing feel.

**"Swingin" in Cut Time**

This new rudiment uses the 16th note triplet. Count the triplet as you would 8th note triplets in cut time.

**The Ratamacue**

**Rudimental Etude #17**

The Single Ratamacue    The Double Ratamacue    The Triple Ratamacue

# The Finish Line!

From "A Fresh Approach to the Snare Drum" by Mark Wessels
International Copyright Secured 1994   All Rights Reserved

# Appendix

This appendix is designed to give the student extra practice on new material covered in each lesson. These exercises are repetitive in nature so that the student can concentrate on the technical aspects of drumming without having to devote most (or all) of his or her attention to rhythm reading.

TEACHERS:  Here are a few suggestions for working with the exercises that are included in the Appendix:

- **<u>Always</u> work with a metronome or accompaniment tracks to ensure a steady tempo!** (Actually, since all of these exercises are in 4/4 time, I use a mobile device with some of my favorite tunes). Try to vary the tempos as much as possible! Beginning percussionists often get buried in the "80 b.p.m." rut and can't play real band music at common tempos because it is foreign to them.

- **Use these exercises as a review to previous lessons.** It only takes two minutes to play through a page (without repeats), so my class will play through the 2 or 3 lessons previous to the one I'm working on as part of their daily warm-up routine.

- **To develop ensemble skills,** try playing a few lines in a round, or pick odd-even lines for the students to play as a duet. Beginning percussionists are often distracted when they hear other parts being played (particularly when they are playing one-on-a-part in their band music). This will help build concentration and give them confidence to play their own part even when another percussionist is playing totally different music.

- **Use different dynamic levels.** Percussionists must learn <u>by practice</u> that dynamics cannot affect the tempo. If you play along with the accompaniment track, have the students match the output level as you adjust the volume knob. This type of practice will teach students that listening and adjusting volume levels is also an important part of being a true percussionist!

# Appendix

## Lesson 2

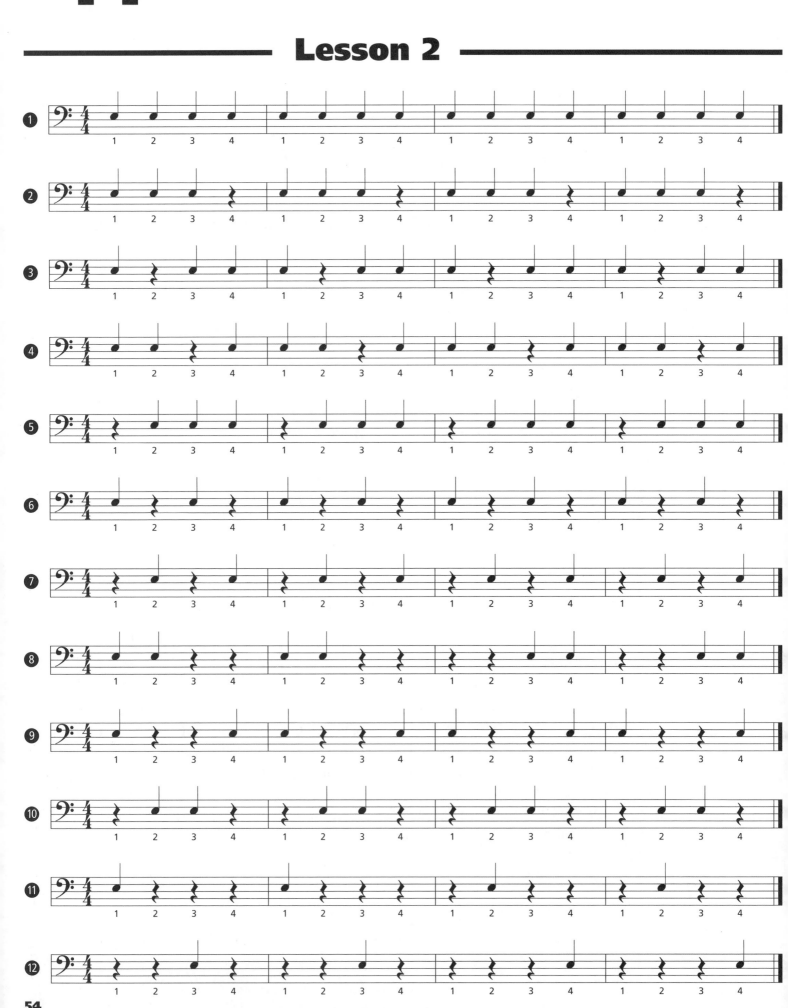

# Lesson 3

# Appendix

## Lesson 4

56

# Lesson 5

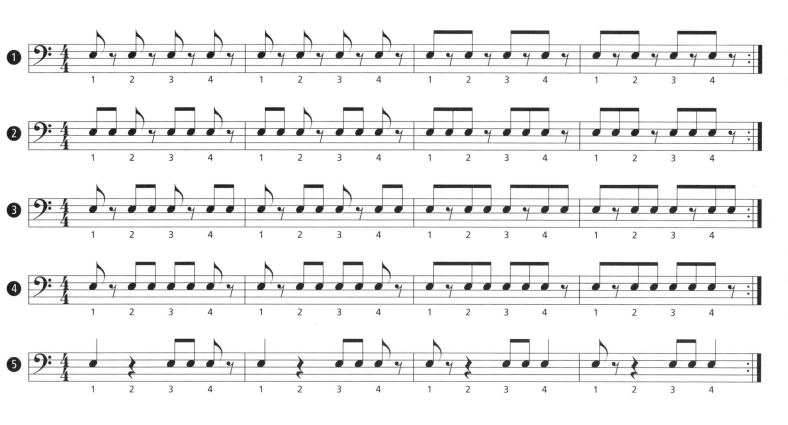

## 8th Rests on the Downbeat

# Appendix

## Lesson 5 continued

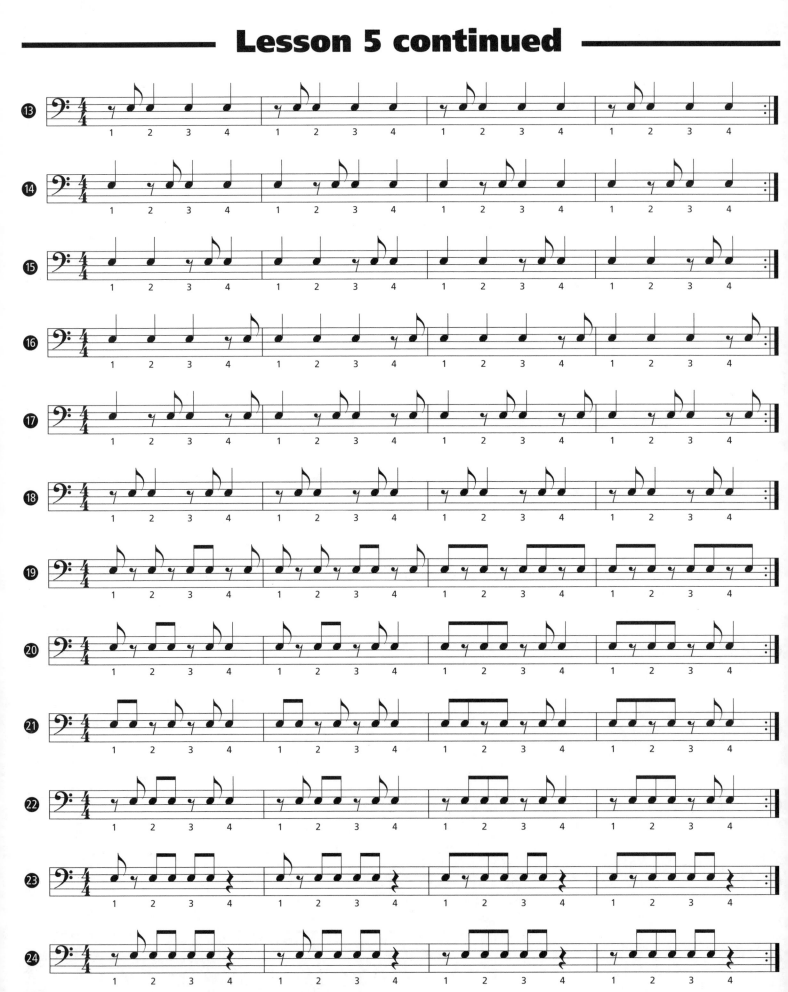

# Lesson 6

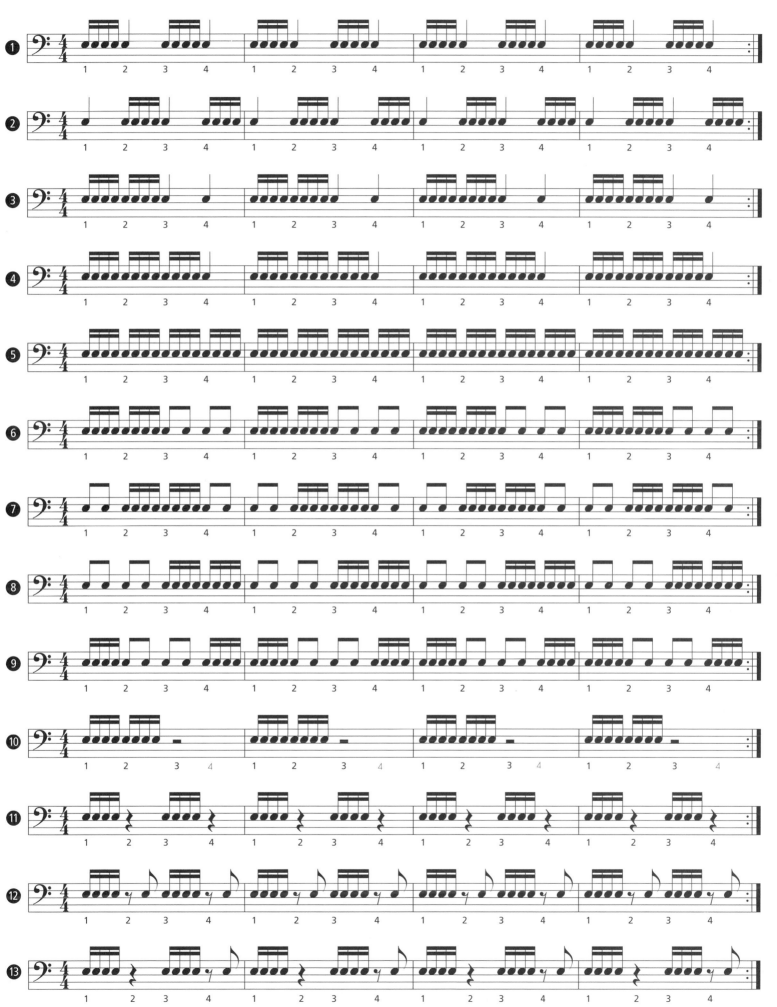

# Appendix

## Lesson 7

## Lesson 8

# Lesson 8 continued

# Lesson 9

# Appendix

## Lesson 10

## Lesson 11

# Lesson 12

# Lesson 13

# Appendix

## Lesson 14

# Lesson 14 continued

# Lesson 15

# Appendix

## Lesson 16

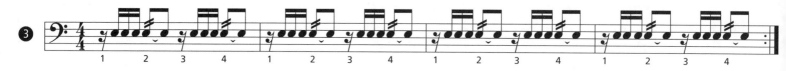

## Lesson 17

# Lesson 18

# Lesson 19

# Appendix

## Lesson 19 continued

## Lesson 20

# Accessory Percussion

All well-rounded percussionists should know the fundamental techniques for the accessory percussion instruments. Included in these two pages is some very basic information followed by an etude that incorporates most of the common techniques. For a more thorough explaination, check out the video lessons that are available for these and other accessory instruments at **www.youtube.com/user/FreshApproachBooks.**

### Concert Bass Drum

The first step in getting a great concert bass drum sound is using a mallet that is generally matched to the size of the bass drum itself. Timpani or keyboard mallets are not large enough to produce a full, deep sound from the drum, so always use a bass drum mallet designed for the drum.

On a bass drum that is in a vertical position, stand slightly to the right side and behind the drum. You will play the drum with your right hand and use your left to muffle the drum head. Strike the drum slightly off center. A stand that allows the drum to be tilted at an angle provides a better playing position for the performer.

If extra muffling is required (for marches and very staccato passages), drape a small towel over the edge of the rim of the drum. Clipping the towel to the rim will keep it in place.

When playing rolls on the bass drum, always use two mallets. Play the roll with alternating single strokes.

## Concert Bass Drum Etude

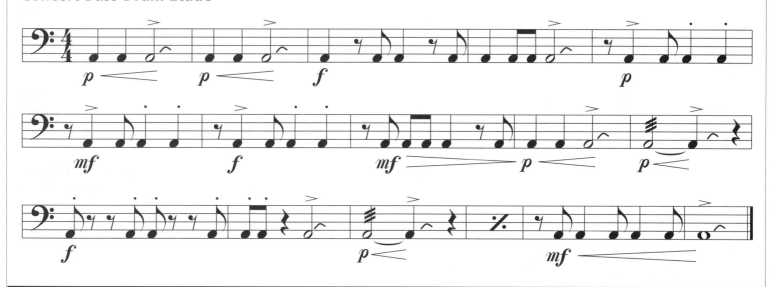

### Crash Cymbals

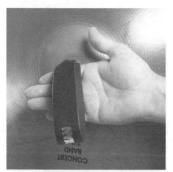

The cymbal straps are held in much the same grip as the right hand snare grip. Let the strap drape over the second joint of the index finger. The fingers then curl around the strap to make a fist.

In order to play a full cymbal crash, one cymbal (usually the left) is held stationary. The right cymbal is held at a slightly higher angle and is dropped down against the left with a "glancing blow." After the cymbals are struck together, bring your hands apart and down slightly so that the cymbals may be allowed to vibrate freely.

For fast, repeated cymbal strikes (as in a march), keep the cymbals close together, with all edges even. Keep the left cymbal stationary and strike it with the left. Usually, time does not permit the "glancing blow" type of strike described above. Keeping one cymbal slightly off–center from the other will usually eliminate air pockets that may occur.

When muffling the cymbals, the follow through is omitted and the edges should be drawn to the players body (chest, midriff, or shoulders) to stop the sound. This is absolutely necessary for short, **staccato** notes. The shorter the notes, the faster the player needs to draw the cymbals to his or her body.

If the crash cymbals are to be played for extended periods of time, have a cymbal rack or padded table to lay the cymbals on when they are not being played.

## Crash Cymbal Etude

## Tambourine

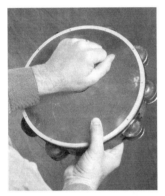

For slow, loud passages, the tambourine is held at about eye level, head side up. The tambourine is then struck with the fist (or fingers) of the opposite hand near the center of the head. To achieve softer dynamics, strike the tambourine with the fingers of the opposite hand near (or on) the rim.

For fast rhythmic passages, the knee must first be raised by placing the foot on a chair or stool. The tambourine is then held head side down and struck alternately against the knee and the fist of the opposite hand.

A **shake roll** is produced by shaking the tambourine using an oscillating wrist action. In order to produce a "clean" start to the roll, strike the instrument in the manner previously described. If the tambourine roll has a release note also, strike the tambourine at the end of the roll.

## Tambourine Etude

Webster's Dictionary describes technique as "The skill or command in handling fundamentals." Developing technique, or the skill of playing the snare drum fundamentals is just as important as learning about notes and rhythms! Below is a chart of the suggested technique exercises and rudiments that correspond to each lesson in the book, along with recommended tempo markings.

**EXERCISES**

| | | | | | | | |
|---|---|---|---|---|---|---|---|
| Lesson 1 | #1 ♩=90 | | | | | | |
| Lesson 2 | #1 ♩=90 | #2 ♩=90 | | | | | |
| Lesson 3 | #1 ♩=100 | #2 ♩=100 | #3 ♩=120 | #4 ♩=120 | | | |
| Lesson 4 | #1 ♩=110 | #4 ♩=140 | #5 ♩=140 | #6 ♩=140 | | | |
| Lesson 5 | #1 ♩=120 | #4 ♩=160 | #5 ♩=160 | #6 ♩=160 | #7 ♩=180 | | |
| Lesson 6 | #1 ♩=126 | #5 ♩=85 | #8 ♩=100 | #9 ♩=85 | | | |
| Lesson 7 | #1 ♩=128 | #5 ♩=90 | #8 ♩=110 | #9 ♩=90 | #10 ♩=100 | | |
| Lesson 8 | #1 ♩=132 | #5 ♩=95 | #8 ♩=120 | #9 ♩=95 | #10 ♩=120 | | |
| Lesson 9 | #1 ♩=134 | #5 ♩=98 | #8 ♩=130 | #9 ♩=98 | #10 ♩=130 | #11 ♩=60 | |
| Lesson 10 | #1 ♩=136 | #5 ♩=102 | #8 ♩=140 | #9 ♩=102 | #11 ♩=70 | #12 ♩=90 | |
| Lesson 11 | #1 ♩=144 | #5 ♩=110 | #8 ♩=144 | #9 ♩=110 | #11 ♩=72 | #12 ♩=100 | #13 ♩=70 |
| Lesson 12 | #1 ♩=148 | #8 ♩=144 | #9 ♩=120 | #11 ♩=72 | #12 ♩=105 | #13 ♩=70 | #14 ♩=120 |
| Lesson 13 | #1 ♩=152 | #8 ♩=148 | #9 ♩=126 | #11 ♩=76 | #13 ♩=80 | #14 ♩=130 | #15 ♩=60 |
| Lesson 14 | #1 ♩=156 | #8 ♩=148 | #9 ♩=130 | #11 ♩=80 | #14 ♩=140 | #15 ♩=64 | #16 ♩=70 |
| Lesson 15 | #1 ♩=162 | #8 ♩=154 | #9 ♩=132 | #14 ♩=145 | #15 ♩=68 | #16 ♩=80 | #17 ♩.=70 |
| Lesson 16 | #1 ♩=174 | #8 ♩=80 | #9 ♩=134 | #14 ♩=150 | #16 ♩=90 | #17 ♩.=80 | #18 ♩=100 |
| Lesson 17 | #1 ♩=178 | #8 ♩=82 | #9 ♩=136 | #14 ♩=160 | #17 ♩.=100 | #18 ♩=110 | #19 ♩=90 |
| Lesson 18 | #1 ♩=180 | #8 ♩=84 | #14 ♩=170 | #17 ♩.=120 | #18 ♩=120 | #19 ♩=96 | #20 ♩=70 |
| Lesson 19 | #1 ♩=182 | #8 ♩=86 | #14 ♩=180 | #18 ♩=140 | #19 ♩=102 | #21 ♩=140 | #22 ♩.=70 |
| Lesson 20 | #1 ♩=184 | #8 ♩=88 | #14 ♩=200 | #18 ♩=160 | #19 ♩=110 | #22 ♩.=80 | #23 ♩=80 |

# TECHNIQUE WORKOUT:
# EXERCISES

These sticking exercises work on the relaxed rebound stroke described on page 6. Strive for an even volume and consistent tempo from right to left hand.

## Exercise #1: "8 On A Hand"

R R R R   R R R R   L L L L   L L L L

## Exercise #2: "Stick Control 1"

R L R R   L R L L   R L R R   L R L L
R L L R   L R R L   R L L R   L R R L
R R L R   L L R L   R R L R   L L R L
R L R L   L R L R   R L R L   L R L R
R R R L   R R R L   R R R L   R R R L
L L L R   L L L R   L L L R   L L L R

## Exercise #1B: "4-2-1"

R R R R   L L L L   R R R R   L L L L
R R L L   R R L L   R R L L   R R L L
R L R L   R L R L   R L R L   R L R L

## Exercise #3: "Four & Four Buzzes"

This exercise works on the multiple bounce, described on page 9. Try to make each bounce "bleed" into the next stroke for a smooth buzz sound.

R L R L   R L R L   R L R L   R L R L

## Exercise #4: "Four & Four Doubles"

These exercises should be used to develop a relaxed double stroke. While seated, lay your hands on your leg & practice **Exercise A** using just your wrists. Each stroke should be very relaxed – with no arm motion at all! Once you develop quick, relaxed doubles on each hand separately, move to **Exercise B**.

**A**

R R   R R   R R   R R   L L   L L   L L   L L

Practice this exercise with your hands on your legs, or with your sticks on a pillow (or something that offers no rebound at all). Strive for a smooth motion from measure one to measure two, with only the wrists and fingers creating the second stroke. Above all else, STAY RELAXED!

**B**

R L R L   R R L L R R L L   R L R L   R R L L R R L L
L R L R   L L R R L L R R   L R L R   L L R R L L R R

## Exercise #5: "Isolated Double Strokes"

This is another exercise that works on the double stroke – this time isolating each hand one at a time, then putting them back together. The same techniques apply: use very relaxed wrist and finger motions to produce the double stroke, but DO NOT BOUNCE THE STICK. Great sounding rolls are achieved only with the ability to use wrist and fingers on double strokes.

R R L R L   R R L R L    R L L R L   R L L R L

R R L   R R L   R R L   R R L    R L L R   L L R   L L R   L L

# TECHNIQUE WORKOUT: EXERCISES

### Exercise #6: "Stick Control 2"

This is a more difficult exercise to develop control over rebound strokes using various sticking patterns. Stay relaxed and listen for a consistent sound from hand to hand. Watch that the quarter notes are given their precise rhythmic value (don't rush them)! Play measure 1 & 2 three times, then meas. four & five.

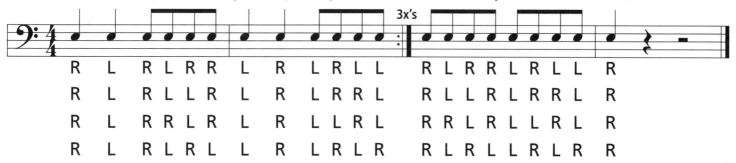

| R | L | R | L | R | R | L | R | L | R | L | L | R | L | R | R | L | R | L | L | R |
| R | L | R | L | L | R | L | R | L | R | R | L | R | L | L | R | L | R | R | L | R |
| R | L | R | R | L | R | L | L | R | L | L | R | L | R | R | L | R | L | L | R | L | R |
| R | L | R | L | R | L | L | R | L | R | L | R | R | L | R | L | L | R | L | R | R |

### Exercise #7: "Mr. Freeze"

Use this exercise to work on downstrokes (described on page 9), taps (described on page 14) and upstrokes (described on page 11). Squeeze the stick slightly on each downstroke to control the rebound and "freeze" the stick 2 inches above the drum, then *immediately* relax the hand for the taps and upstroke. Play the taps as soft, relaxed wrist strokes (2–3 inches), then lift on the upstroke to prepare for the next downstroke.

| R | R | R | R | R | R | R | R | R | R | L | L | L | L | L | L | L | L | L | L |
| DOWN | tap | tap | tap | tap | up | DOWN | tap | tap | tap | tap | up | DOWN | tap | tap | tap | tap | up | DOWN | tap | tap | tap | tap | up |

### Exercise #8: "Bucks in Three"

Using the same basic technique as Exercise #7. Strive to play the exercise at two heights: 12 inches (a "full" stroke) for the accent and 2–3 inches for the tap and upstroke. Remember: let the weight of the forearm and wrist take care of the volume of the accent! Don't use any more tension than is necessary!

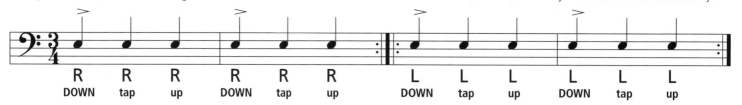

| R | R | R | R | R | R | L | L | L | L | L | L |
| DOWN | tap | up | DOWN | tap | up | DOWN | tap | up | DOWN | tap | up |

### Exercise #9: "Extended Doubles"

ONLY practice this exercise with your hands on your legs or with the sticks on a pillow! Stay relaxed, but do not allow the stick to bounce.

| R L R L R R L L R R L L | R L R L R R L L R R L L | R R L L R R L L R R L L R R L L | R |
| L R L R L L R R L L R R | L R L R L L R R L L R R | L L R R L L R R L L R R L L R R | L |

### Exercise #10: "Flam Prep"

Use this exercise to isolate the soft, relaxed grace notes of the flam as described in Lesson 7. Remember: two heights – 12 inches for the PRIMARY stroke, 2 inches for the grace notes. Exercise C should be played with an upstroke motion on the final grace note to prepare for the flam on the opposite hand.

| A | L L L R | L L L R | B | R R R L | R R R L | C | L L L R | R R R L |

74

# TECHNIQUE WORKOUT: EXERCISES

### Exercise #11: "Alternating Accents"

This exercise works on the same two height concept as Exercise #7, this time throwing in some taps BETWEEN the downstrokes and upstrokes. Watch the motion that is made on the 8th notes, then strive for the same motion on the 16ths. Listen for a consistent sound on ALL of the innerbeats.

### Exercise #12: "16th Note Timing"

Work with a metronome and strive for rhythmic accuracy on this exercise. Maintain a relaxed REBOUND stroke all the way through. Use a full stroke at the slowest tempo, then slightly lower the stick heights as you increase the speed.

### Exercise #13: "Roll Prep"

Unlike the double strokes in the previous exercises, this one applies the BOUNCE technique described on Lesson Eleven. Maintain a consistent motion of the hands throughout. **Exercise A** works on the double bounce (or "open" roll), **Exercise B** uses the multiple bounce ("buzz") roll.

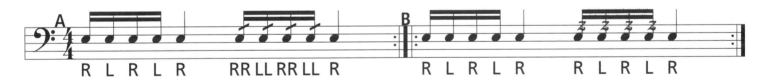

### Exercise #14: "Grid Diddles"

This exercise uses a simple "grid" pattern to isolate single hand diddles. The diddle shifts on the four note "grid," from the first note, to the second, to the third, etc. At a slow tempo, use the wrist and fingers to produce a controlled double STROKE. Faster tempos require a double BOUNCE.

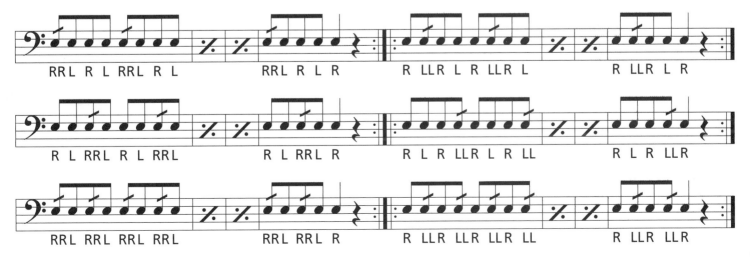

# TECHNIQUE WORKOUT: EXERCISES

### Exercise #15: "Flam Control"

Use this exercise to develop control over alternating flams. The motion that is used in the first measure is EXACTLY THE SAME as the motion in the second. Practice playing the primary stroke of the flam in the air just above the drum (sometimes called a "fake flam") to develop control over the downstroke.

R R R R R R R R   R L R L R L R     L L L L L L L L   L R L R L R L R

### Exercise #16: "Chicken and a Roll" ☆

Work for an even motion from the 16th notes to the bounces. Count the "roll skeleton" out loud to ensure a consistent tempo. Use double bounce as well as multiple bounce rolls and practice starting on the left as well as the right.

R L R L R   R L R L R   R L R L R L R L R   R
L R L R L   L R L R L   L R L R L R L R L   L

### Exercise #17: "Alternating Accents in Three"

This is another two height exercise. Play each accent with a full stroke and innerbeats at 2–3 inches. Practice playing this exercise in the air above the drum to gain control over the downstrokes. See how close you can come to hitting the drum without actually doing it!

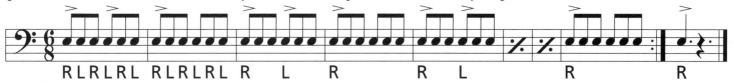

R L R L R L   R L R L R L   R   L   R   R   L   R   R

### Exercise #18: "Grid Flams"

Using the same "grid" concept as "Grid Diddles."  The first measure in each segment isolates the accent pattern, then you'll add the flam in the second. Watch your sticking very carefully! Even with the flam shifting from downbeat to upbeat, the sticking remains consistent.

R L R L R L R L   R L R L R L R L   R L R L R L R L   R L R L R L R L

R L R L R L R L   R L R L R L   R L   R L R L R L R L   R L R   L R L R   L   R

### Exercise #19: "Chicken & a Tap Roll" ☆

R L R L R   R L R L R   R L R L R L R L R

R L R L R L R L R L R L R L R L   R L R L R L R L R L   R

# TECHNIQUE WORKOUT:
# EXERCISES

### Exercise #20: "Flam Tap Rebound"

As the speed increases on Flam Taps, it becomes necessary to play rebound strokes instead of controlled strokes. Use a full stroke on the accent, but allow the stick to rebound for the second and third notes. The third note becomes the grace note for the opposite hand flam.

### Exercise #21: "Flam Accents and Single Drags"

Use this exercise to isolate the alternating motion of the hands on Flam Accents and Single Drags.

### Exercise #22: "Flams, Drags and Rolls"

The two height motion in the first measure should be exactly the same in the second. Play the accents at 9 inches and taps at 3.

### Exercise #23: "Triplet Timing"

This exercise works on the rhythmic timing of triplet patterns. Play at a consistent volume level with REBOUND strokes.

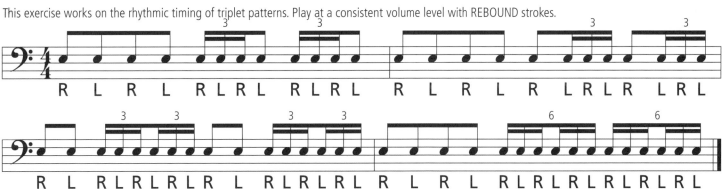

# RUDIMENT PROGRESS CHART

The rudiments below are listed in the order in which they appear in the book. The tempos marked refer to the BRONZE, SILVER and GOLD level play-along tracks included on the DATA CD (i.e. "B1" = Bronze level, 1st tempo; "B2"= Bronze level, 2nd tempo, etc.). Rudiments notated with an asterisk (*) are not formally introduced in the book, but since the techniques are similar to what is covered in other rudiments, it's recommended that you learn these as well.

| Rudiment | Lesson 1 | Lesson 2 | Lesson 3 | Lesson 4 | Lesson 5 | Lesson 6 | Lesson 7 | Lesson 8 | Lesson 9 | Lesson 10 | Lesson 11 | Lesson 12 | Lesson 13 | Lesson 14 | Lesson 15 | Lesson 16 | Lesson 17 | Lesson 18 | Lesson 19 | Lesson 20 |
|---|---|---|---|---|---|---|---|---|---|---|---|---|---|---|---|---|---|---|---|---|
| Single Stroke Roll (#1) | B1 | B1 | B2 | B3 | B4 | S1 | S1 | S2 | S2 | S3 | S3 | S4 | S4 | G1 | G1 | G2 | G2 | G3 | G3 | G4 |
| Double Stroke Roll (#6) | B1 | B1 | B1 | B2 | B2 | B3 | B3 | B4 | B4 | S1 | S2 | S2 | S3 | S3 | S4 | G1 | G2 | G3 | G4 | G5 |
| Multiple Bounce Roll (#4) |  | B1 | B1 | B2 | B2 | B3 | B3 | B4 | B4 | S1 | S1 | S2 | S2 | S3 | S3 | S4 | G1 | G2 | G3 | G4 |
| 5 Stroke Roll (#7) |  |  |  | B1 | B1 | B2 | B2 | B3 | B3 | B4 | S1 | S2 | S2 | S3 | S4 | G1 | G2 | G3 | G4 | G5 |
| Single Stroke Four (#2) |  |  |  | B1 | B1 | B2 | B2 | B3 | B3 | B4 | B4 | S1 | S1 | S2 | S3 | S4 | G1 | G2 | G3 | G4 |
| Single Paradiddle (#16) |  |  |  |  | B1 | B1 | B2 | B3 | B4 | B5 | S1 | S2 | S3 | S4 | S5 | G1 | G2 | G3 | G4 | G5 |
| 9 Stroke Roll (#10) |  |  |  |  | B1 | B2 | B2 | B3 | B3 | B4 | S1 | S2 | S2 | S3 | S4 | G1 | G2 | G3 | G4 | G5 |
| 13 Stroke Roll (#13) |  |  |  |  |  | B1 | B2 | B3 | B3 | B4 | S1 | S2 | S2 | S3 | S4 | G1 | G2 | G3 | G4 | G5 |
| Flam (#20) |  |  |  |  |  | B1 | B1 | B2 | B3 | B4 | B5 | S1 | S2 | S3 | S4 | S5 | G1 | G2 | G3 | G4 |
| Flam Tap (#22) |  |  |  |  |  |  | B1 | B2 | B3 | B4 | B5 | S1 | S2 | S3 | S4 | S5 | G1 | G2 | G3 | G4 |
| Single Stroke Seven (#3) |  |  |  |  |  |  |  |  | B1 | B2 | B3 | B4 | S1 | S2 | S3 | S4 | G1 | G2 | G3 | G4 |
| Flam Paradiddle (#24) |  |  |  |  |  |  |  |  |  | B1 | B3 | B5 | S1 | S2 | S3 | S5 | G1 | G2 | G3 | G4 |
| Double Paradiddle (#17) |  |  |  |  |  |  |  |  |  |  | S1 | S2 | S3 | S4 | S5 | G1 | G2 | G3 | G4 | G5 |
| * Triple Paradiddle (#18) |  |  |  |  |  |  |  |  |  |  | S1 | S2 | S3 | S4 | S5 | G1 | G2 | G3 | G4 | G5 |
| * Paradiddle-diddle (#19) |  |  |  |  |  |  |  |  |  |  | S1 | S2 | S3 | S4 | S5 | G1 | G2 | G3 | G4 | G5 |
| 17 Stroke Roll (#15) |  |  |  |  |  |  |  |  |  |  |  | S1 | S2 | S3 | S4 | G1 | G2 | G3 | G4 | G5 |
| Flamacue (#22) |  |  |  |  |  |  |  |  |  |  |  |  | B1 | B3 | B5 | S2 | S4 | G1 | G3 | G4 |
| Drag (#31) |  |  |  |  |  |  |  |  |  |  |  |  |  | B1 | B3 | S1 | S3 | G1 | G3 | G4 |
| Drag Paradiddle #2 (#37) |  |  |  |  |  |  |  |  |  |  |  |  |  |  | B3 | S1 | S3 | G1 | G3 | G4 |
| * Drag Paradiddle #1 (#26) |  |  |  |  |  |  |  |  |  |  |  |  |  |  |  | B3 | S1 | S3 | G1 | G3 |
| 7 Stroke Roll (#9) |  |  |  |  |  |  |  |  |  |  |  |  |  |  |  | S3 | S4 | G1 | G3 | G4 |
| Lesson 25 (#34) |  |  |  |  |  |  |  |  |  |  |  |  |  |  |  |  | S3 | G1 | G3 | G4 |
| Single Drag (#32) |  |  |  |  |  |  |  |  |  |  |  |  |  |  |  |  |  | S1 | S3 | G1 |
| Flam Accent (#21) |  |  |  |  |  |  |  |  |  |  |  |  |  |  |  |  |  |  | S1 | G1 |
| Single Drag, Triplet (#32) |  |  |  |  |  |  |  |  |  |  |  |  |  |  |  |  |  |  | S1 | G1 |
| 5 Stroke Roll, Triplet (#7) |  |  |  |  |  |  |  |  |  |  |  |  |  |  |  |  |  |  | S1 | G1 |
| Single Ratamacue (#38) |  |  |  |  |  |  |  |  |  |  |  |  |  |  |  |  |  |  |  | G1 |
| Double Ratamacue (#39) |  |  |  |  |  |  |  |  |  |  |  |  |  |  |  |  |  |  |  | G1 |
| Triple Ratamacue (#40) |  |  |  |  |  |  |  |  |  |  |  |  |  |  |  |  |  |  |  | G1 |

# ESSENTIAL RUDIMENTS

The following are the 40 International Drum Rudiments as adopted by the Percussive Arts Society, along with level designations that you can use to track your progress. The play-along tracks for each of the 40 rudiments are available in the "Rudiments" folder on the DATA CD. Rudiments marked with an asterick (*) should also be played with a LEFT HAND LEAD sticking.

## I. ROLL RUDIMENTS

### 1. Single Stroke Roll

R L R L R L R L R L R L R L R L

| BRONZE | | | | SILVER | | | | GOLD | | | |
|---|---|---|---|---|---|---|---|---|---|---|---|
| 50 | 60 | 70 | 80 | 90 | 100 | 110 | 120 | 130 | 140 | 150 | 160 |

### 2. Single Stroke Four

R L R L   R L R L   *

| BRONZE | | | | SILVER | | | | GOLD | | | |
|---|---|---|---|---|---|---|---|---|---|---|---|
| 65 | 70 | 75 | 80 | 85 | 90 | 95 | 100 | 105 | 110 | 115 | 120 |

### 3. Single Stroke Seven

R L R L R L R   L R L R L R L

| BRONZE | | | | SILVER | | | | GOLD | | | |
|---|---|---|---|---|---|---|---|---|---|---|---|
| 65 | 70 | 75 | 80 | 85 | 90 | 95 | 100 | 105 | 110 | 115 | 120 |

### 4. Multiple Bounce Roll

| BRONZE | | | | SILVER | | | | GOLD | | | |
|---|---|---|---|---|---|---|---|---|---|---|---|
| 20 | 30 | 40 | 50 | 60 | 70 | 80 | 90 | 100 | 110 | 120 | 130 |

### 5. Triple Stroke Roll

R R R L L L R R R L L L

| BRONZE | | | | SILVER | | | | GOLD | | | |
|---|---|---|---|---|---|---|---|---|---|---|---|
| 50 | 55 | 60 | 65 | 70 | 75 | 80 | 85 | 90 | 95 | 100 | 105 |

### 6. Double Stroke Open Roll

R R L L R R L L etc.

| BRONZE | | | | SILVER | | | | GOLD | | | |
|---|---|---|---|---|---|---|---|---|---|---|---|
| 40 | 45 | 50 | 55 | 60 | 65 | 70 | 75 | 80 | 85 | 90 | 95 | 100 |

### 7. Five Stroke Roll

also

R R L L   R L R L R L

| BRONZE | | | | SILVER | | | | GOLD | | | |
|---|---|---|---|---|---|---|---|---|---|---|---|
| 40 | 45 | 50 | 55 | 60 | 65 | 70 | 75 | 80 | 85 | 90 | 95 | 100 |

*(Triplet Variation)*

| BRONZE | | | | SILVER | | | | GOLD | | | |
|---|---|---|---|---|---|---|---|---|---|---|---|
| 70 | 75 | 80 | 85 | 90 | 95 | 100 | 105 | 110 | 115 | 120 | 125 | 130 | 135 | 140 |

### 8. Six Stroke Roll

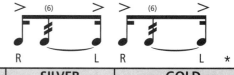

R L R L *

| BRONZE | | | | SILVER | | | | GOLD | | | |
|---|---|---|---|---|---|---|---|---|---|---|---|
| 40 | 45 | 50 | 55 | 60 | 65 | 70 | 75 | 80 | 85 | 90 | 95 | 100 |

### 9. Seven Stroke Roll

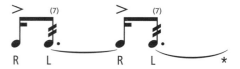

R L R L *

| BRONZE | | | | SILVER | | | | GOLD | | | |
|---|---|---|---|---|---|---|---|---|---|---|---|
| 40 | 45 | 50 | 55 | 60 | 65 | 70 | 75 | 80 | 85 | 90 | 95 | 100 |

### 10. Nine Stroke Roll

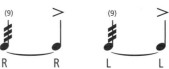

R R L L

| BRONZE | | | | SILVER | | | | GOLD | | | |
|---|---|---|---|---|---|---|---|---|---|---|---|
| 40 | 45 | 50 | 55 | 60 | 65 | 70 | 75 | 80 | 85 | 90 | 95 | 100 |

### 11. Ten Stroke Roll

R L R L R L R L R L R L *

| BRONZE | | | | SILVER | | | | GOLD | | | |
|---|---|---|---|---|---|---|---|---|---|---|---|
| 70 | 75 | 80 | 85 | 90 | 95 | 100 | 105 | 110 | 115 | 120 | 125 | 130 | 135 | 140 |

### 12. Eleven Stroke Roll

R L R L R L R L R L R L *

| BRONZE | | | | SILVER | | | | GOLD | | | |
|---|---|---|---|---|---|---|---|---|---|---|---|
| 70 | 75 | 80 | 85 | 90 | 95 | 100 | 105 | 110 | 115 | 120 | 125 | 130 | 135 | 140 |

### 13. Thirteen Stroke Roll

R R L L

| BRONZE | | | | SILVER | | | | GOLD | | | |
|---|---|---|---|---|---|---|---|---|---|---|---|
| 40 | 45 | 50 | 55 | 60 | 65 | 70 | 75 | 80 | 85 | 90 | 95 | 100 |

### 14. Fifteen Stroke Roll

R L R L *

| BRONZE | | | | SILVER | | | | GOLD | | | |
|---|---|---|---|---|---|---|---|---|---|---|---|
| 40 | 45 | 50 | 55 | 60 | 65 | 70 | 75 | 80 | 85 | 90 | 95 | 100 |

### 15. Seventeen Stroke Roll

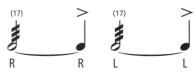

R R L L

| BRONZE | | | | SILVER | | | | GOLD | | | |
|---|---|---|---|---|---|---|---|---|---|---|---|
| 40 | 45 | 50 | 55 | 60 | 65 | 70 | 75 | 80 | 85 | 90 | 95 | 100 |

# ESSENTIAL RUDIMENTS

## II. PARADIDDLE RUDIMENTS

### 16. Single Paradiddle

R L r R L r L L

| BRONZE | | | | | BRONZE | | | | | GOLD | | | | |
|---|---|---|---|---|---|---|---|---|---|---|---|---|---|---|
| 30 | 35 | 40 | 45 | 50 | 55 | 60 | 65 | 70 | 75 | 80 | 85 | 90 | 95 | 100 |

### 17. Double Paradiddle

R L R L R R L R L R L L

| BRONZE | | | | | BRONZE | | | | | GOLD | | | | |
|---|---|---|---|---|---|---|---|---|---|---|---|---|---|---|
| 30 | 35 | 40 | 45 | 50 | 55 | 60 | 65 | 70 | 75 | 80 | 85 | 90 | 95 | 100 |

### 18. Triple Paradiddle

R L R L R L R R L R L R L R L L

| BRONZE | | | | | BRONZE | | | | | GOLD | | | | |
|---|---|---|---|---|---|---|---|---|---|---|---|---|---|---|
| 30 | 35 | 40 | 45 | 50 | 55 | 60 | 65 | 70 | 75 | 80 | 85 | 90 | 95 | 100 |

### 19. Paradiddle-Diddle

R L R R L L R L R R L L
L R L L R R L R L L R R

| BRONZE | | | | | BRONZE | | | | | GOLD | | | | |
|---|---|---|---|---|---|---|---|---|---|---|---|---|---|---|
| 30 | 35 | 40 | 45 | 50 | 55 | 60 | 65 | 70 | 75 | 80 | 85 | 90 | 95 | 100 |

## III. FLAM RUDIMENTS

### 20. Flam

L R      R L

| BRONZE | | | | | BRONZE | | | | | GOLD | | | | |
|---|---|---|---|---|---|---|---|---|---|---|---|---|---|---|
| 30 | 35 | 40 | 45 | 50 | 55 | 60 | 65 | 70 | 75 | 80 | 85 | 90 | 95 | 100 |

### 21. Flam Accent

L R L R   R L R L

| BRONZE | | | | | BRONZE | | | | | GOLD | | | | |
|---|---|---|---|---|---|---|---|---|---|---|---|---|---|---|
| 30 | 35 | 40 | 45 | 50 | 55 | 60 | 65 | 70 | 75 | 80 | 85 | 90 | 95 | 100 |

### 22. Flam Tap

L R R R L L L R R R L L

| BRONZE | | | | | BRONZE | | | | | GOLD | | | | |
|---|---|---|---|---|---|---|---|---|---|---|---|---|---|---|
| 30 | 35 | 40 | 45 | 50 | 55 | 60 | 65 | 70 | 75 | 80 | 85 | 90 | 95 | 100 |

### 23. Flamacue

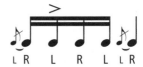
L R L R L L R      *

| BRONZE | | | | | BRONZE | | | | | GOLD | | | | |
|---|---|---|---|---|---|---|---|---|---|---|---|---|---|---|
| 30 | 35 | 40 | 45 | 50 | 55 | 60 | 65 | 70 | 75 | 80 | 85 | 90 | 95 | 100 |

### 24. Flam Paradiddle

L R L R R R L R L L

| BRONZE | | | | | BRONZE | | | | | GOLD | | | | |
|---|---|---|---|---|---|---|---|---|---|---|---|---|---|---|
| 30 | 35 | 40 | 45 | 50 | 55 | 60 | 65 | 70 | 75 | 80 | 85 | 90 | 95 | 100 |

### 25. Flammed Mill

L R R L R R L L R L

| BRONZE | | | | | BRONZE | | | | | GOLD | | | | |
|---|---|---|---|---|---|---|---|---|---|---|---|---|---|---|
| 30 | 35 | 40 | 45 | 50 | 55 | 60 | 65 | 70 | 75 | 80 | 85 | 90 | 95 | 100 |

### 26. Flam Paradiddle-Diddle

L R L R R L L R L R L L R R

| BRONZE | | | | | BRONZE | | | | | GOLD | | | | |
|---|---|---|---|---|---|---|---|---|---|---|---|---|---|---|
| 30 | 35 | 40 | 45 | 50 | 55 | 60 | 65 | 70 | 75 | 80 | 85 | 90 | 95 | 100 |

### 27. Pataflafla

L R L R R L R R L R R L *

| BRONZE | | | | | BRONZE | | | | | GOLD | | | | |
|---|---|---|---|---|---|---|---|---|---|---|---|---|---|---|
| 30 | 35 | 40 | 45 | 50 | 55 | 60 | 65 | 70 | 75 | 80 | 85 | 90 | 95 | 100 |

### 28. Swiss Army Triplet

L R R L L R R L

| BRONZE | | | | | BRONZE | | | | | GOLD | | | | |
|---|---|---|---|---|---|---|---|---|---|---|---|---|---|---|
| 30 | 35 | 40 | 45 | 50 | 55 | 60 | 65 | 70 | 75 | 80 | 85 | 90 | 95 | 100 |

### 29. Inverted Flam Tap

L R L R L R L R L R L R

| BRONZE | | | | | BRONZE | | | | | GOLD | | | | |
|---|---|---|---|---|---|---|---|---|---|---|---|---|---|---|
| 30 | 35 | 40 | 45 | 50 | 55 | 60 | 65 | 70 | 75 | 80 | 85 | 90 | 95 | 100 |

### 30. Flam Drag

L R L L R R L R R L

| BRONZE | | | | | BRONZE | | | | | GOLD | | | | |
|---|---|---|---|---|---|---|---|---|---|---|---|---|---|---|
| 30 | 35 | 40 | 45 | 50 | 55 | 60 | 65 | 70 | 75 | 80 | 85 | 90 | 95 | 100 |

## IV. DRAG RUDIMENTS

31. Drag

L L R     R R L

| BRONZE | | | | SILVER | | | | GOLD | | | |
|---|---|---|---|---|---|---|---|---|---|---|---|
| 45 | 50 | 55 | 60 | 65 | 70 | 75 | 80 | 85 | 90 | 95 | 100 |

36. Drag Paradiddle #1

R L L R L R R L R R L R L L

| BRONZE | | | | SILVER | | | | GOLD | | | |
|---|---|---|---|---|---|---|---|---|---|---|---|
| 45 | 50 | 55 | 60 | 65 | 70 | 75 | 80 | 85 | 90 | 95 | 100 |

32. Single Drag Tap

L L R   L R R L   R    *also*   R L R L R L

| BRONZE | | | | SILVER | | | | GOLD | | | |
|---|---|---|---|---|---|---|---|---|---|---|---|
| 45 | 50 | 55 | 60 | 65 | 70 | 75 | 80 | 85 | 90 | 95 | 100 |

37. Drag Paradiddle #2

R L L R L L R L R R L R R L R R L R L L

| BRONZE | | | | SILVER | | | | GOLD | | | |
|---|---|---|---|---|---|---|---|---|---|---|---|
| 45 | 50 | 55 | 60 | 65 | 70 | 75 | 80 | 85 | 90 | 95 | 100 |

33. Double Drag Tap

L L R L L R   L R R L R R L   R

| BRONZE | | | | SILVER | | | | GOLD | | | |
|---|---|---|---|---|---|---|---|---|---|---|---|
| 45 | 50 | 55 | 60 | 65 | 70 | 75 | 80 | 85 | 90 | 95 | 100 |

38. Single Ratamacue

L L R L R L   R R L R L R

| BRONZE | | | | SILVER | | | | GOLD | | | |
|---|---|---|---|---|---|---|---|---|---|---|---|
| 45 | 50 | 55 | 60 | 65 | 70 | 75 | 80 | 85 | 90 | 95 | 100 |

34. Lesson 25

R L L R L   R L L R L   *

| BRONZE | | | | SILVER | | | | GOLD | | | |
|---|---|---|---|---|---|---|---|---|---|---|---|
| 45 | 50 | 55 | 60 | 65 | 70 | 75 | 80 | 85 | 90 | 95 | 100 |

39. Double Ratamacue

L L R L L R L R L R R L R R L R L R

| BRONZE | | | | SILVER | | | | GOLD | | | |
|---|---|---|---|---|---|---|---|---|---|---|---|
| 45 | 50 | 55 | 60 | 65 | 70 | 75 | 80 | 85 | 90 | 95 | 100 |

35. Single Dragadiddle

R R L R R   L L R L L

| BRONZE | | | | SILVER | | | | GOLD | | | |
|---|---|---|---|---|---|---|---|---|---|---|---|
| 45 | 50 | 55 | 60 | 65 | 70 | 75 | 80 | 85 | 90 | 95 | 100 |

40. Triple Ratamacue

L L R L L R L L R L R L R R L R R L R R L R L R

| BRONZE | | | | SILVER | | | | GOLD | | | |
|---|---|---|---|---|---|---|---|---|---|---|---|
| 45 | 50 | 55 | 60 | 65 | 70 | 75 | 80 | 85 | 90 | 95 | 100 |

# DRUMSET FUNDAMENTALS

All percussionists should know how to play the drumset. This section, adapted from "A FRESH APPROACH TO THE DRUMSET," will get you playing along to some great tracks in no time! And with the FREE video lessons available, you can learn by watching world-renowned drummer Stanton Moore demonstrate all the fundamentals!

For FREE drumset video lessons, go to ☞ www.youtube.com/user/FreshApproachBooks

## Learn About the Parts of the Drumset

Crash Cymbal
Ride Cymbal
Mounted Toms (or Rack Toms)
Hi-Hat Cymbals
Snare Drum
Floor Tom
Cymbal Boom Stand
Hi-Hat Stand
Bass Drum
Pedals

## Cymbals

While the drums are the heart of the drumset, the cymbals provide the color. There are 3 general areas to play on: The Crash Area, Ride Area and Bell. Every set should have at least three types of cymbals:

RIDE: The ride is the largest and heaviest of the three. Generally, you'll play time-keeping patterns on the ride cymbal.

CRASH: These are smaller, thinner cymbals that you'll use to "punch" parts of the music.

HI-HAT: The hi-hat cymbals come in pairs and you'll play them with either your foot (via the hi-hat pedal) or your hands.

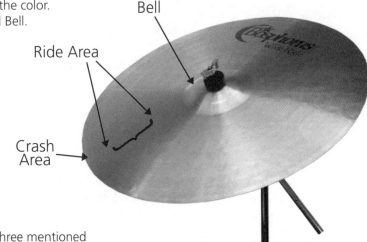

Bell
Ride Area
Crash Area

There are many other types of cymbals available in addition to the three mentioned above – chinas, sizzles, splashes as well as a dizzying array of other metallic sounds.

# Setting Up the Drumset

## The Throne

Often young drummers will use chairs or stools that do not adjust to the proper position for playing the drumset so having a good drum throne is important. Adjust your throne height so that your legs are above parallel to the floor and the heels are below the knees.

## The Snare Drum

The height of the snare drum should be a few inches ABOVE your legs. Adjust the tilt of your drum so that it offers a level playing surface.

## Bass Drum and Hi-Hat

Start with a comfortable snare drum position and move the bass drum pedal and hi-hat to you. The foot pedals should be in a position where the feet naturally fall.

Once the bass drum pedal is in a comfortable position, slide the bass drum in to meet the pedal. This way you will be setting up the bass drum to fit your body, not the other way around.

## Mounted Toms

Position your toms in front of your snare with a slight angle toward you. Try to get them as close as possible without the rims touching. Avoid extreme angles as this will affect the sound you get from the drum.

## Floor Tom

The floor tom should be within easy reach – roughly the same height as the snare drum, with a slight angle towards you. Be sure to leave a comfortable amount of space for your leg.

## Crash Cymbal

The crash cymbal is usually placed to the left of the toms, within easy reach of the right AND left hands. Adjust the stand height so that the cymbal does not make contact with the tom when it's played.

## Ride Cymbal

The ride cymbal is placed a few inches above and to the right of the 2nd tom. You should be able to reach the ride with the right hand without extending your elbow.

# Foot Technique on the Bass Drum and Hi-Hat

## Heel Down

This technique is generally preferred by drummers who want control on low volume and expressive playing. To play with the heel down technique, simply play your right foot while leaving the heel touching the footplate.

## Heel Up

The heel up technique is preferred by drummers who want the greatest volume. With this technique, play by lifting the leg and dropping the foot to the floor – or by suspending the leg in the air while you play the pedal with the ball of the foot.

## Open Tones and Dead Tones

An OPEN TONE is achieved by allowing the beater to rebound off the drum head – similar to a snare drum rebound stroke. This allows the bass drum head to vibrate freely and achieves the most resonant sound from the drum.

A DEAD TONE is played by "burying the beater" into the drum head. This type of stroke has the maximum punch and attack, but the least resonance because the batter head isn't allowed to vibrate.

## Hi-Hat Pedal Technique

Most drummers use both the heel up and heel down techniques on the hi-hat: HEEL DOWN when playing open hi-hat sounds with the sticks – and HEEL UP when playing left foot hi-hat "chick" sounds.

The bass drum is notated in the bottom space of the staff. When the hi-hat is played with the left foot, it is notated beneath the staff.

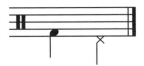

# Sticks on the Hi-Hat

To play the hi-hat with the sticks, start by depressing the pedal so the hi-hat cymbals are in the "closed" position. The hi-hat can be played with the tip or the shaft of the stick – each creates a unique sound (the tip is used for lighter sounds, the shaft for heavier sounds).

Most drummers play "right-over-left" on hi-hat/snare patterns, although playing the left hand on the hi-hat (called "open handed playing") offers many advantages as well. Experiment with each hand on the hi-hat and find what works best for you.

# Beginning Independence

  Look for this play-along track in the "drumset" folder on the mp3 cd!

Start by counting "1, 2, 3, 4" out loud while you play the top line (x) on the hi-hat with one hand, then add your opposite hand on the snare drum playing the bottom notes. Once you have that down, play the bass drum with the hi-hat part instead of the snare!

*The play-along track alternates between 4 times with hi-hat/snare, then 4 times hi-hat/bass. You can also play it by alternating between the snare and bass EVERY measure – while keeping a consistent tempo on the hi-hat!*

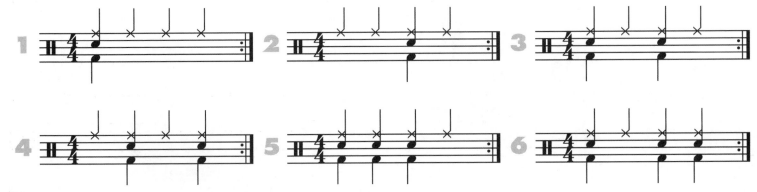

# "ROCK STAR"

Your first drum beat is easy to learn – and it's been played by some great drummers on countless hit records! The right hand will play steady beats on all four counts while you alternate between bass drum and snare drum beats.

Start slowly and count out loud as you play. Practice the groove over and over until you can play with steady relaxed strokes. After you can get a consistent sound and feel, try playing it with the play-along track.

repeat this groove
for the entire song!

Count:   1 & 2 & 3 & 4 &   1 & 2 & 3 & 4 &

 There are two play-along tracks – one WITH drums and one WITHOUT drums. To play along with the "drumless" track, you'll need to listen closely to the bass player and keep a steady tempo!

# 8th Notes on the Hi-Hat

**Watch the FREE video lessons!**
www.youtube.com/user/FreshApproachBooks

 Work for a consistent, relaxed hi-hat sound and make sure that all of the notes hit precisely together in tempo.

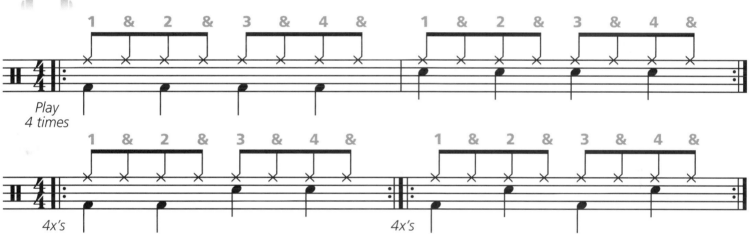

Play
4 times

4x's                    4x's

# 8th Note Rock Beats

Try to get different sounds on each of these grooves – from a soft, tight hi-hat sound with the tip of the stick, to a loud, trashy, open sound with the shaft of the stick. Listen carefully to the groove and strive to put every note "in the pocket."

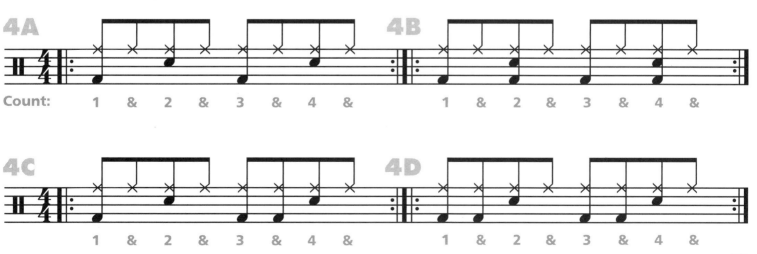

# The Ride Cymbal

The "RIDE CYMBAL" was named for the "ride" (time-keeping) patterns that are often played on it. A general "all-purpose" playing area for the ride cymbal is about a third of the way in from the edge.

## Ride Cymbal Grip ("French Grip")

When you begin to reach around the drumset, it often helps to rotate your hand slightly so you can minimize the movement of your arms. The grip you'll use on the ride (most commonly referred to as the "FRENCH GRIP") is produced by turning your hand to where the thumb is on top of the stick, as if you were going to shake hands.

For more ride cymbal sounds, you can also play on the bell (also called the "dome").

Or you can play with the shoulder of the stick on the edge for a heavy crash. A good ride cymbal can be played as a crash as well.

## "SOLID AS A ROCK"

Watch Stanton jam to this track! www.youtube.com/user/FreshApproachBooks

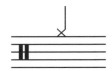

 This track switches from the hi-hat at Letter A to the ride cymbal at Letter B. Drummers will often play a beat on the hi-hat during the "verse" (letter A), then move to the ride during the "chorus" to get a bigger sound. If you're up for a challenge on the chorus, try playing your left foot hi-hat on 2&4 with the snare!

Play 3 times

count: **2** & 2 & 3 & 4 & **3** & 2 & 3 & 4 &

# The Crash Cymbal

The crash cymbal is used to punch the beginning of a musical phrase or to add a big finish to the end of a drum "fill". A cymbal crash is usually played with the shoulder of the stick on the edge of the cymbal.

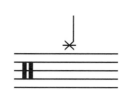

Practice this exercise with a metronome so you can learn to play a cymbal crash without loosing tempo in the groove.

# The Toms

As you learn to play the toms, it's important to stay relaxed, using as little forearm motion as necessary. While drummers have a wide range in the number of toms they use, the most common "5 piece" drum kit uses two "rack" toms and a floor tom:

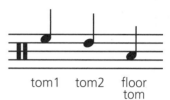

tom1   tom2   floor tom

Here are a couple of drum grooves that add toms. Experiment with playing open-handed (left hand on the hi-hat), or moving the right hand to the ride cymbal.

6A          6B

> These are just a sample of the huge number of beats and fills available in the full version of A FRESH APPROACH TO THE DRUMSET! Ask for it at your local music store or purchase it online:
> **http://www.mwpublications.com**

# Drum Fills

Drummers often set up new musical phrases with a DRUM FILL – providing some rhythmic variety to the beat with the snare, toms, bass drum and cymbals. The goal of the drum fill is to bridge the gap, or lead one phrase into the next. Here is an example of a 2 count fill played at the end of a four measure phrase.

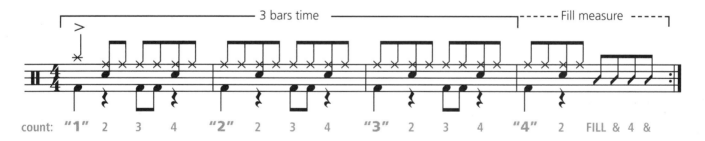

One of the easiest ways to come up with fill ideas is to take a rhythm pattern and explore all the possible ways to play it. Here are a few ways you can play a simple 2 count fill using four 8th notes:

7A          7B          7C

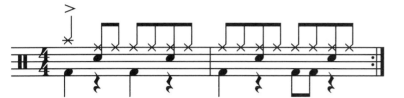

# "SOLID TIME"

This tune has an "AB" form (moving between the verse and chorus), with an added intro. Take a few minutes to learn the beats in the verse and chorus separately before trying to play the whole tune. Work with a metronome at a slow tempo until the groove feels good, then gradually increase the speed of the metronome until you can play it with the play-along track.

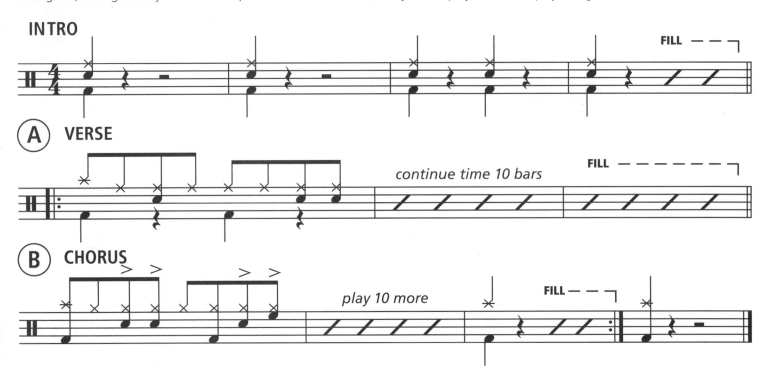

## Having fun yet?

You're just getting started! All of these lessons were adapted from "A Fresh Approach to the Drumset" – and you've barely scratched the surface of what you can learn!

Best of all, you can download instructional videos with world-renowned drummer and educator STANTON MOORE. Available for your computer, iPad, iPhone or Android device – it's a great way to have fun learning to play the drumset!

Check it out now at
# http://www.mwpublications.com!